SONG OF
SOLOMON
MAKE FULL MY JOY

SONG OF SOLOMON

MAKE FULL MY JOY

God's Model for Your Marriage

DON ANDERSON

LOIZEAUX BROTHERS
Neptune, New Jersey

First Edition, September 1987

Printed in the United States of America

A publication of Loizeaux Brothers, Inc.
A nonprofit organization devoted to the Lord's work and to the spread of
His truth.

Library of Congress Cataloging-in-Publication Data
Anderson, Don, 1933-
  Song of Solomon.
  Bibliography: p.
  1. Bible. O.T. Song of Solomon—Commentaries.
2. Marriage—Biblical teaching. I. Title.
BS1485.3.A53 1987   223'.9077   87-2807
ISBN 0-87213-002-9

The author wishes to acknowledge the editorial assistance of Jane Rod-
gers.

Dedication

To my wife, Pearl, who has been a priceless pearl to me. It was she who wrote this poem, entitled "Walk within Thy House with a Perfect Heart."

Lord, how I long to serve Thee upon some great
   missionfield
And have the world see how much I love Thee
By this sacrifice.
"Nay," came His voice so gentle, yet so firm.
"Walk within thy house with a perfect heart
"And do not for other things yearn."

Then Lord make within these walls,
A perfect sacrifice of Thy grace.
A place where all who enter
May see Thy face
And rest and be renewed.

May those who dwell here, Lord,
Find always warm welcome, peace, and happy
   words.
That when they go, their own hearth to build,
They will have a perfect pattern,
And Thy perfect will fulfill.

אֲנִי לְדוֹדִי וְדוֹדִי לִי

I am my beloved's, and my beloved is mine
Song of Solomon 6:3

πάντα χαὶ ἐν πᾶσιν Χφισός.

Christ is all and in all
Colossians 3:11

Contents

Foreword

Is my father qualified to write a book on marriage? Although some may claim that being his eldest child makes me prejudiced, I'd have to say, "Of course!" But before I tell you why, I must toss sibling rivalry aside and mention that I'm not just speaking for myself, but for my brothers and sisters also. Our parents' marriage has been an inspiration to us all.

Perhaps one of the most inspiring truths about our folks' relationship is that it has not been perfect. Thanks to these imperfections, we kids were given a realistic picture of married life—and a supernatural picture of the God who works in the lives of Christian husbands and wives.

While we were growing up, our parents consistently and wholeheartedly tried to ready us for our own marriages. I remember that when I was in junior high, Mom, Dad, and I began to pray for the man I would marry—whoever he might be. We asked God to prepare my future husband for me, and me for him.

From this experience with my folks, I learned that a good marriage does not just happen. It requires prayerful preparation. That lesson has not been forgotten, either. Today, as a married woman, I still pray about my relationship with my husband, asking the Lord to enable our love to grow and our commitment to endure.

Commitment has long been the name of the game for Mom and Dad. It was not always easy for them to keep their marriage a high priority, especially with the demands of five children and a full-time ministry. Yet through the years, we saw first-hand our parents' day-to-day commitment to each other, pervading everything they did. The key ingredient for them has been—and remains—their solid belief in the authority of Scripture and in the truth of God's principles concerning marriage, so many of which are given in the Song of Solomon. When problems arose, when things seemed to grow cold, our parents made the choice to believe and follow God's will and way.

The beautiful part of the story is that now, with all five of us kids grown and out on our own, our parents are reaping the benefits of the commitment they made long ago to keep the spark of their love alive. It is a joy for us to see them and to learn from their example.

Since God is the key to marital success, I hope that you will be excited and challenged at the opportunity to study the Song of Solomon, His textbook revealing His design and desires for wedded love. May this book be a blessing to you and your marriage.

DONNA ANDERSON SKORHEIM
for the five of us

Preface

Dare we label a book of Scripture as unsuitable for public consumption? Ridiculous, you say! And yet through the years many have done very nearly that with the Song of Solomon. David Hocking writes of the Song in his book, *Romantic Lovers:*

> As a young boy I was told by older Christians that it was not good to read the book until I was much older. When I got older, I found that many Christians were not sure that the book should be taught or spoken about in public! (Hocking 1986, 7).

What a disquieting, disturbing statement! As men and women of God, we do not have the option of picking and choosing which sections of the Bible to explore and which to ignore, or which to teach and which to avoid. God gave us the entire canon of Scripture for our instruction and edification. In the words of the apostle Paul to his coworker Timothy, "All Scripture is inspired by God and profitable for teaching, for reproof, for correction, for training in righteousness; that the man of God may be adequate, equipped for every good work" (2 Timothy 3:16-17 NASB). Note that it is all, not simply part, of God's Word which is good for us!

Do We Take It at Face Value?

Although all Scripture is profitable to us, there has been much neglect of the Song of Solomon in years past. Part of the problem centers on methods of interpreting the book.

Debate has focused on the following questions: Should the Song be interpreted literally, as the picture of a godly relationship between a man and a woman within the bond of marriage? Is it an allegory depicting the love of God for the nation Israel? Is it a symbolic portrait of the union of Christ and His bride, the church? As Ironside points out in his commentary on the Song:

> We may think of the book from four standpoints. Looking at it literally, we see the glorification of wedded love. Looking at it from a dispensational standpoint, we see the relationship between Jehovah and Israel. Redemptively, we find the wonderful relationship between Christ and the Church. And studying it from the moral or spiritual standpoint, we see it as the book of communion between an individual soul and the blessed, glorified, risen Lord (Ironside 1981, 11).

Until the past few decades, most scholars who have dealt with the Song of Solomon have not interpreted the text literally—in Ironside's words, as the "glorification of wedded love." In fact, one finds almost as many different interpretations of the Song as there are interpreters! Yet why should we consider the Song on any except a literal level? The material is sensitive in nature, yes, but isn't it logical that God would include a model for our earthly marriage within His holy Word? And surely the sensual language used by the speakers in the Song proves that what is depicted there is a relationship between a man and a woman, and nothing else!

A CASE FOR STRAIGHTFORWARD INTERPRETATION

The golden rule of biblical interpretation is that when the plain sense makes good sense, seek no other sense. Unger says it well:

> Therefore, take every word at its primary, usual, literal meaning, unless it is patently a rhetorical figure

or unless the immediate context, studied carefully in the light of related passages and axiomatic and fundamental truths, clearly points otherwise (Unger, 176).

When considered as the literal portrait of a husband and wife, the Song makes perfect sense. There is no need to seek another meaning.

The crux of the dilemma centers around one's attitude toward the laws of interpretation themselves. However, I suggest that with our limited human knowledge, we really have *no choice* but to consider Scripture literally, accepting that God means directly what He says. Reading between the lines, dissecting the Word for obscure meanings and messages, is risky business because we are human and therefore capable of making mistakes. Indeed, only eternity will reveal the degree to which biblical truth has been distorted by well-intentioned interpreters who have departed from the plain, normal, straightforward interpretation of scriptural text.

The Song of Solomon is not the only section of Scripture where interpretation has proved controversial over the years. Bible prophecies have confounded many a student of the Word. Again and again the question has arisen: Should we take literally what is predicted in Scripture, believing that what God tells us will happen is going to take place? The answer must be *yes!* Just as the plagues recorded in Exodus were real, so will the plagues predicted in Revelation 6–19 come to pass. Four-fifths of all biblical prophecy has already been specifically fulfilled; it is a certainty that the final fifth will come true also. We can count on it and we should live our lives in expectation of it, if we truly accept Bible prophecy literally.

Acceptance of scriptural truth at face value is essential. After all, as Christians we stake our eternal destiny on the literal fact that Christ was God in flesh who came to this earth to die for us, taking upon Himself our sins. His was no symbolic suffering, but a tangible payment of the penalty for our disobedience.

Besides, God gave His Word to us to be understood and

interpreted by the normal laws of language. As Charles Ryrie puts it in *Basic Theology:*

> To sum up: It is God who desired to give man His Word. It is God who also gave the gift of language so He could fulfill that desire. He gave us His Word in order to communicate, not confound. We should seek to understand that communication plainly, for that is the normal way human beings communicate (Ryrie 1986, 115).

THE ULTIMATE MARRIAGE MANUAL

We risk missing the dynamic, life-changing truths of Scripture when we ignore the obvious and search for hidden meanings and allegorical fancies. Just as it is deadly to reject the fact that Christ's death and resurrection were anything but literal events, and foolish to doubt that God's final judgment so graphically pictured in the Revelation will one day take place, it is tragic to overlook the principles of marriage vividly portrayed in the Song of Solomon. Failing to see the Song as a literal, poetic portrait of a godly marriage relationship means missing out on many of God's guidelines for matrimony!

Because the Song has frequently not been seen for what it really is—God's marriage manual for His children—many writers, even Christian ones, have strayed from Scripture to seek answers to marital problems from secular sources. And yet such departures are unnecessary because God deals with the important issues of the marriage relationship directly in His Word. All we need do is examine the biblical text plainly and then apply its lessons to our own lives.

As we begin our own study of the Song, we are taking the literal, straightforward approach in exploring the text. May I invite you to read on and discover how real, how relevant, how romantic Solomon's lyric of love truly is?

Taking the Plunge

I now pronounce you husband and wife," the minister proclaims in a voice loud enough even for Great-grandma Smith to catch, without turning up the volume on her hearing aid. Then, with a faint, knowing smile, the man of God gently nods to the groom and quietly says, "You may now kiss your bride."

The flower girl stops fidgeting and stares up expectantly. Camera shutters click as the nervous twenty-four-year-old husband, clad in a rented tuxedo for the first time since his senior prom, lifts the lacy blusher of his new wife's veil. He grasps her left hand and touches his lips to hers. Grinning broadly, they turn to face their guests. The bride's pink-gowned maid of honor hands back the bouquet and stoops to straighten the train of the expensive wedding gown. Then to the strains of the recessional, the pair marches back down the aisle and into the reality of life together. They are officially one—on paper, at least.

Yet as a minister who has performed nearly three hundred weddings . . . and counseled hundreds of couples who have become disenchanted with their marriages, I can tell you that much more is involved in becoming one than making it through the wedding ceremony, as complicated as even that may be in our age of lavish receptions and high-priced photographers. One-becoming can be very unbecoming, at times.

As soon as our spit-polished young pair exits the church, they enter a lifelong process of adjustment and adaptation. It begins quickly, possibly as soon as the receiving line forms at the reception.

I remember a story told by two of my good friends, a

young couple on the executive board of our ministry. It seems that at the dinner following their wedding, their fathers were standing together, chatting. "How does Sally handle money?" asked the groom's dad.

"She still has the first nickel she ever earned," replied the father of the bride. "What about John?"

"Spends every dime he can lay his hands on," chuckled the new husband's father. And if it wasn't apparent before, both men knew then that the wedding was simply the beginning of some difficult steps toward oneness for their children.

Thankfully, the young man and woman have bridged much of their economic gap, but their story illustrates that marriage is the product of the joining of two unique personalities, two distinct individuals. Husband and wife must somehow learn to understand each other, to change when necessary, to accept freely, and to forgive generously.

THE GRAND, THE GRIND, THE GROAN . . . AND THE GROWTH

Many marriages (including my own) undergo a series of phases. I call these the grand, the grind, the groan, and the growth. Under normal circumstances, everything is wonderful in the beginning, after the wedding bells first chime. The typical newlyweds sweep each other off their feet with a display of love and affection which can only be classified as grand. Flowers, candy, cards, calls, and candlelight dinners are common. For most couples, the romantic fires of love will probably burn with flaming ardor during the first year or so of wedded bliss. The ecstasy is sheer and sure!

Gradually the bonfire may dim, though not without sending up an occasional flare as it wanes. Then the cold shower of reality hits as kids arrive, bills mount, mortgages accrue, promotions occur, committee work increases, church obligations expand, and life generally becomes hectic and complex. Almost inevitably, the grand begins to seem more like a grind.

Along the way, many husbands and wives become disenchanted with their mates, weary of their commitments, sick of their responsibilities. The grind becomes a groan in the hearts of two one-time lovers, a long, drawn-out wail of disappointment and shattered dreams. Alarmingly, the dirty word *divorce* enters the conversation; the discouraged pair sees splitting up as a viable alternative to what has proved to be a bum deal. Indeed, with the pressures on modern marriages, it is a wonder any couple manages to remain happily wedded. Too often even Christians merely stay together out of a sense of obligation, not because they are truly content with each other. The flavor, fervor, and fire are gone from the relationship.

It doesn't have to be that way. There is another option which I hope you will consider as you read this book. God did not design marriage as a lifelong punishment, a venture into mutual agony. He planned it as a state in which a man and a woman could find complete fulfillment. He intends it as a catalyst for growth—and it is with that goal in view that we must proceed.

It is a law of life, whether physical or spiritual, that growth comes through change. Spiritually, growth takes place as the Spirit of God conforms us more and more to the image of Christ. The apostle Paul speaks of this process of change in Romans 12:2: "Don't let the world around you squeeze you into its own mold, but let God remold your minds from within, so that you may prove in practice that the plan of God for you is good, meets all his demands and moves toward the goal of true maturity" (Phillips). In our marriage, the challenge to each of us is to make a common commitment to change, allowing God to help us communicate more honestly with our partner and to care more deeply for his or her welfare than for our own. As we do that, we'll enter the growth phase. Our marriage won't just bloom; it will flourish. As husbands and wives, we'll grow together, and as an added bonus, we'll find ourselves becoming more like Christ in the process.

How-To?

How can a relationship survive the grand, the grind, and the groan, and enter the growth stage? May I suggest referring to the greatest how-to manual of all time, the Bible, for that answer? Scripture is the ultimate textbook on marriage. God's Word abounds with principles and practical insights concerning the commitment of a husband and a wife. We will observe such biblical guidelines as we consider the Song of Solomon, exploring the beautiful love relationship of the king and his bride Shulamith, the country girl from Lebanon. The book is an evocative and literal description of married love.

Before we examine the inspired wisdom of Solomon, we are going to consider what the book of Ruth has to say to us about the nature of love itself. Surprisingly, some of what we'll learn will come from observing the traditionally antagonistic relationship between a mother and her daughter-in-law.

Following our glance at the book of Ruth, we'll turn to the New Testament and explore the words of Philippians 2:1-5. The apostle Paul's comments about human fellowship are particularly pertinent to husbands and wives. There, from the pen of an unmarried man, comes one of the greatest passages in the Word of God which may be practically applied to the marriage relationship. Paul's comments, although not specifically addressed to those who are married, offer wisdom to all who have taken the plunge into wedded life.

Diving In

My wife Pearl and I took that plunge some thirty-three years ago. I'll never forget our wedding day and the feelings I experienced while standing before the minister. I was stunned by the reality of the moment—acutely aware of how ill-prepared I was to undertake that lifelong commitment. Pearl expressed the thoughts of both of us when she said, following the ceremony, "Is this all there is? After all that hoopla, I at least expected to feel different!" But there we were—two scared kids who happened to love each other intensely, and who shared a burning devotion to Jesus Christ. We certainly had a long way to go! We were so much like the young lovers pictured in Ruth Harms Calkin's poem, "Help, Lord!"

On our beautiful sunlit wedding day
I said "I do" with all the devotion
Of my ecstatic heart.
If I had known that day
All that I know now
I would have said "I do"
Just as eagerly, just as joyfully.
But I would have added
One quick secret plea:
"Help, Lord!"

Since our own "beautiful sunlit wedding day," Pearl and I have come a long way. As I was reflecting on our years together, I remembered a counseling situation which took place a number of months ago. The couple with whom I was talking had been married for many years. In the heat of the moment, the wife blurted out, "This makes me so mad! We have been married long enough that we ought to be a blessing to each other by now!"

I'm thankful that Pearl and I have reached the point in our relationship where we are a blessing to each other—most of the time, that is. Our arrival there hasn't come easily. As we've trudged through the years, dragging five kids in tow, we have experienced it all: the grand, the grind, the groan, and the growth. Now if we can just survive the empty nest syndrome, we'll soon cross the Jordan and enter the land of eternal rest and blessing!

In the meantime, to all my readers who are weary in the fight, may I recommend the words of Jesus in Matthew 11:28-30:

Come to Me, all who are weary and heavy-laden, and I will give you rest. Take My yoke upon you, and learn from Me, for I am gentle and humble in heart; and you shall find rest for your souls. For My yoke is easy, and My load is light (NASB).

And may the sections of Scripture which we're going to look at now, minister to you and to your marriage as dynamically as only God's Word can.

Part One

Laying the Foundation

The Definition of Love

Ruth 1–4

In the beginning, God created the world and He created man. Then He rested. But man wasn't complete—in all the earth there was not found "a helper suitable for him" (Genesis 2:18 NIV). So God created woman . . . and cynics say that neither God nor man has rested since!

Yet what would the human race be without women? Scarce, for one thing . . . but in all seriousness, my own life has been made immeasurably richer because I have shared it with a woman I love deeply—my wife, Pearl. Anyone who knows us can tell you how much I depend upon her. She is a source of strength, a God-given gift without equal, beyond compare.

Pearl and I met while in college. It took me awhile to convince her to marry me, but marry we eventually did—some thirty-three years ago now. It was the best decision I have ever made, other than the time in which I invited Christ into my life. I think Pearl would agree.

As it did with us, the love of a man and a woman frequently leads to marriage in our society. That reminds me of a story I once heard. It seems a rabbi and a Roman Catholic priest were seated together at a banquet. The main course was, much to the rabbi's chagrin, baked ham. Said the priest to the rabbi, "Why don't you try that ham? It's delicious—U.S.D.A. Choice Inspected."

Replied the rabbi to the priest, "Are you married?"

"No," came the answer.

"Try it," retorted the rabbi. "It's better than ham."

And it is! Apparently other folks share the sentiments of

the rabbi, because weddings are on the increase, even in our age of modern "morality" and live-in lovers.

But even though weddings are popular, the national divorce rate is rocketing to disturbing heights. Too often love and marriage seem mutually exclusive. It's almost as if the lyrics to the old song ought to be:

> Love and marriage, love and marriage,
> Don't go together like a horse and carriage.
> If you love, why bother?
> You can't have one and the other.

WHY THE MUSIC STOPS

Certainly I'm exaggerating, because many fine, warm, loving marriages exist. Yet too often the ties of matrimony bind together a love grown cold. As someone once said, a marriage can too easily come to resemble an ancient, creaky violin. The strings may still be attached, but the sweet music is gone.

Why does the music turn sour? There are many reasons. To some men, all being married means is that a maid and a mistress are available, all rolled into one. To put it bluntly, it's clean socks in the morning and sex at 10:00 P.M. It's nearness without closeness, cohabitation without communication or cooperation. Few women could be happy with that sort of arrangement over the long haul. And yet it is surprising how often just such a dismal state of affairs exists. Below is an example typical of many couples whom I have counseled in my years of ministry.

"I go to work and she takes care of the house," said one husband whose wife suffered from bouts of depression. She spent her days mopping up basins and bathtubs, wiping runny noses, changing dirty diapers, preparing meals, ironing shirts. Her man would come home, plant a perfunctory kiss on her lips (or maybe just her cheek), pat the baby, tousle the hair of the two-year-old, and then peruse the evening newspaper till dinner. After the meal and the obligatory fifteen minutes of interaction with the children, hubby generally switched on the television while the little woman cleaned up the dishes. He would watch *Monday Night Football* or the cable sports network while she bathed the kids, put them to bed, then collapsed on the sofa. Of course when it was time for the "happy" couple to go to bed, he was ready to make love, and she, exhausted, would do her best to comply. No wonder she was depressed! Her husband did not participate actively in her life or in the routine of the home. He was merely a boarder with bedroom privileges. She felt unappreciated and misunderstood. And she was.

Don't Look at Me!

Before we continue, let me make it clear that I am not a psychologist or psychiatrist, but a pastor and teacher. God has given me the opportunity over the past thirty years to counsel many couples whose marriages have hit rockbottom. In that time I've been able to make a few observations. What follows are reflections based on what I have seen and heard.

It is interesting that, by and large, most of the men I've counseled involved in troubled marriages do not seem to feel that they have significantly contributed to the problems in their home. "If she'd just shape up, we could live together," exclaimed an exasperated husband in one of our many sessions. He could not see that his hyper-critical attitude and refusal to genuinely share himself with his wife and kids had steered their relationship onto a collision course with disaster.

There seems to be a tendency to place women on trial when marriages falter. "It is the wife's fault." But at the base of many a crumbling relationship sits a perfectionist husband, insensitive to the needs and desires of the woman he married. Husband and wife are familiar, but not truly intimate. Theirs is a union of sorts, without any real communion.

That reminds me of the old story of Mr. Perfect and his wife, a lady who struggled every waking hour to please him. Never had she been able to escape a critical comment from him, no matter what she did or how hard she tried. One morning he ordered eggs for breakfast—one fried and one scrambled. She rushed diligently into the kitchen in order to prepare them. She concentrated on her task whole-heartedly, carefully heating the skillet, melting the butter, and fixing the eggs just as he had asked. She slid them onto a platter, added hot biscuits, grits, and gravy, and placed them before his waiting majesty.

"Hmmph," was all he said, staring at the eggs on his plate. "You blew it again. You scrambled the wrong one!" I guess some women can never win, considering the men they have to live with!

Of course wives are often accessories in the crime of marriage murder. Unrealistic expectations, indifference, impatience—these may jointly or separately help kill a relationship. For a wife with fairy-tale expectations, the handsome prince she married is doomed to wind up as a toad in the end, incapable of fulfilling even a fraction of her carping demands.

The result? Frequently the lovely young woman our imperfect prince married degenerates into the seven A.M. spectacular, shuffling around the kitchen in slippers and a kimono, barking signals like a seal. What a pleasure to wake up to!

ALL YOU NEED IS LOVE?

So much for stereotypes. There is not enough space in this book to catalog every reason why marriages fail. I believe that there is, however, a cause of marital crisis which is common in many sagging relationships. To many, marriage—if not a state of constant turmoil—is less than it should be, and I believe that this is partly because of a misunderstanding concerning a central issue. Quite simply, we have forgotten what love really is.

The problems of marriage are the problems of two. At the heart of the matter is love. And love misunderstood spells nothing but trouble.

So let's look at love a moment. I'm not talking about the puppy-love infatuation that two teenagers feel. I'm not talking about a tempestuous romance engulfing two heart-sick college students. The love to which I'm referring is neither mushy nor gushy. It's an act of will in which two individuals pledge themselves to each other for a lifetime. It is durable, flexible, patient, and forgiving. It unifies. In its ideal state, it is what the apostle Paul speaks of in 1 Corinthians 13:4-7:

> Love is patient, love is kind. It does not envy, it does not boast, it is not proud. It is not rude, it is not self-seeking, it is not easily angered, it keeps no record of wrongs. Love does not delight in evil but rejoices with the truth. It always protects, always trusts, always hopes, always perseveres (NIV).

It is the glue which cements two people together for five, six, perhaps even seven decades. In Scripture, we find an amazing picture of the qualities of such love in the Old Testament book of Ruth. The text reminds us of what married love is really all about and challenges us to reevaluate our own relationship in the light of God's wisdom and design.

THE BOOK OF RUTH

The book of Ruth, while written around 1000 B.C., concerns events which took place somewhat earlier, during the period described in the book of Judges. Ruth lived in the days when Israel was governed by a series of judges. It was a turbulent, immoral age—a time not so very different from our own in many ways.

Under Joshua's leadership, the children of Israel had finally successfully entered the land of Canaan. There they subdued the majority of the Canaanite tribes. Pockets of resistance remained and, as we see in the pages of Judges, these peoples were slowly being conquered. We also see in the book of Judges that the Israelites themselves fell into sin. As a nation, they plunged headlong into immorality, disregarding divine absolutes and embracing the worldly, the sensual, and the selfish. It was a time in which, as the final verse of Judges states, "Everyone did what was right in his own eyes" (21:25 NASB).

In other words, everyone acted as a law unto himself. Could anyone live righteously in that kind of a society? As the story of the Gentile woman Ruth shows us, the answer is yes. The story of Ruth, Boaz, and Naomi is strikingly beautiful. Ruth was a fragrant and lovely flower, thriving in the midst of a stagnant and foul-smelling pool. There are always those who look to God, even while living in a decadent culture. Ruth was such a woman.

THE STORY

Chapter 1 of the book of Ruth tells us that a severe famine struck the land of Israel during the time of the judges. Elimelech, his wife Naomi, and their two sons, Mahlon and Kilion, left Bethlehem of Judah and journeyed to the land of Moab to escape the famine. They set up housekeeping, but shortly thereafter everything fell apart. Elimelech died, and Naomi was left with her two sons (1:1-3).

The boys married Moabite women, Orpah and Ruth. Ten years passed, then another devastating blow leveled the family. Both Mahlon and Kilion died. Ruth and Orpah were childless widows, but at least they still lived among their people, the Moabites (1:4-5). Naomi, however, was completely alone. She had lost her husband; her sons were dead; her daughters-in-law were not of her race. She was a stranger in a strange land. So Naomi came to the most logical conclusion possible under the circumstances. She would return to her own people (1:6).

Naomi, Ruth, and Orpah packed their bags, and the trio of women set out for the land of Judah (1:6-7). But then Naomi realized the full implications of the sacrifice her daughters-in-law were preparing to make. "Go back, each

of you, to your mother's home. May the LORD show kindness to you, as you have shown to your dead and to me,"
she told Ruth and Orpah (Ruth 1:8 NIV).

"We will go back with you to your people," the girls
tearfully insisted, even after Naomi had kissed them goodbye (1:10 NIV). Yet why should they? Naomi would never (it
seemed) be able to provide husbands for them. They would
be leaving their homeland, their relatives, their gods. Naomi urged the young women to reconsider. She generously
released them from any guilt or obligation, begging them
to remain behind (1:11-14).

Orpah was convinced. She kissed her mother-in-law and
turned back. But Scripture says that Ruth clung to Naomi.
She refused to let go, uttering these incredible words of love
and loyalty:

> Don't urge me to leave you or to turn back from you.
> Where you go I will go, and where you stay I will stay.
> Your people will be my people and your God my God.
> Where you die I will die, and there I will be buried.
> May the LORD deal with me, be it ever so severely, if
> anything but death separates you and me (Ruth 1:16-
> 17 NIV).

When Naomi saw that Ruth was determined to accompany her, she said no more, and they journeyed on together
(1:18-19).

THE FIRST INGREDIENT: RESPONSIBILITY

Ruth possessed an enormous sense of responsibility for
the mother of the man she had married. She willingly left
her friends and her family. She voluntarily set out for a
foreign country, committing herself to care for an old woman. Her responsibility had not ended with the death of her
husband.

Caring for Naomi may have been an extension of her
obligation to her late husband, yet it is obvious that Ruth

greatly loved the older lady as well. Anyone asking, "Hey Ruth, heard any good mother-in-law jokes lately?" would have been met by a cold stare in return, because no animosity existed between the two. And so from the unlikely combination of mother and daughter-in-law, we find that the first ingredient of biblical love is illustrated, for love involves accepting awesome responsibility. And acceptance of this responsibility can be tough.

A little over three years ago, the Lord brought a very special young man, Ray Devine, into the life of our daughter Becky. They fell deeply in love, and planned to be married. Pearl and I were ecstatic—we felt we had literally prayed that godly young fellow into the picture. He seemed to be the ideal mate for our girl. But before the wedding could take place, I felt it necessary to make sure that Ray understood the full implications of the commitment he would be making.

You see, Becky is severely diabetic. For Ray, marrying her would entail dealing with her medical difficulties. It would mean bills, insulin injections, visits to a host of doctors. Her kidneys were failing—dialysis would be necessary and a transplant was going to eventually be required (Becky has since received a kidney transplant). There was no assurance that their life together would encompass more than a few years. And the probability that they would ever have children of their own was practically nil.

Ray and I discussed all of this in a heart-to-heart talk some time before the wedding. As a father, it was hard for me to speak so candidly—almost clinically—about my little girl, but Pearl and I had to be certain that Ray knew exactly what he would be undertaking when Becky and he repeated their vows. I am proud to say that he never wavered in his decision. He has been a wonderful husband to our daughter, and although they have been through more crises than most of us will ever face, they have been tremendously happy. Ray went into the marriage with his eyes wide open, fully aware of the magnitude of the responsiblity he was assuming. He was willing . . . and ready.

DEFINING THE TERM—A MAN'S HOME IS MORE
THAN HIS CASTLE

Perhaps it would be a good idea, before going any further, to define responsibility in the marriage relationship. "Oh yeah, I'm responsible," muttered a disgruntled husband. "Every time something goes wrong at home, my wife tells me, 'You're responsible!'" But responsibility in marriage doesn't mean just shouldering the blame for the problems. It involves assuming an irrevocable commitment that continues long after the kids are raised, one that is meant to last a lifetime. It means eventually becoming accountable to God for the state of the relationship. And the bulk of the responsibility in any marriage falls upon the man.

When I perform a wedding, I like to include what I call "the transfer of headship" in the ceremony. I tell the groom, "This woman has been the responsibility of her parents. They have trained her up in the way in which she should go. She is now your responsibility. Her welfare, way of life, and quality of life, will be determined by how well you accept that obligation." It's not unusual for the young man to turn a tad pale after hearing those remarks! (None have fled the church, though.)

Why does it seem that I am picking on husbands? I can hear the protests now. Yet my reasoning is simple. In the words of the apostle Paul to the Ephesian Christians, "For the husband is the head of the wife, as Christ also is the head of the church, He Himself being the Savior of the body" (Ephesians 5:23 NASB). Men, we're it! We're the heads. Ultimately, the chickens will come home to roost on top of our receding hairline. It's up to us not to wind up with too much egg on our face in the meantime.

Think of the time in the patriarch Jacob's life when he met the living God. Genesis 32 tells of the time when Jacob, at Peniel, wrestled with the angel of the Lord. At this moment of surrender, he grappled with God Himself. Everyone else had crossed the brook Jabbok; they were out of the picture, and he faced the Lord alone (32:22-32). So, too, will we men confront God Himself someday. The Lord is going to hold us accountable for the state of our home. We'll have to answer for the marriage we've created, the woman we've lived with, the children we've fathered. God has given us this stewardship.

So the point I'm trying to drive home is that if our marriage is not all it should be, we men had better examine ourselves. Are we guilty of being lackadaisical about the goings-on in the home? Are we so caught up in making a living that we tell our wife, either verbally or by our actions, "It's your responsibility to take care of the house and kids; it's mine to make the money"? Do we forget to be sensitive to the fact that the jobs our wife performs around the house and with the children are emotionally and physically draining, and often just plain boring . . . and that the problems are compounded when the need for a second income requires our mate to work outside the home, too? Do we show our appreciation? Do we regularly help out? Or do we spend so much time at the office or on the golf course or at the jogging track that we neglect to participate actively in our own home? If the last statement is true, we are ignoring the glaring reality of our primary obligations.

ENCOURAGING—HAVING A HEART . . . AND SHARING IT!

Let me suggest some positive steps we can take to remedy the situation—and to fulfill the role God intended for us in marriage. First, let's recognize that we have a *responsibility to encourage.* We should energetically look for ways to show our appreciation to those with whom we live.

Many times in couples' conferences put on by our staff, we give this assignment: we ask the husbands and wives to think about one quality they really admire in their spouse. Then we ask each to privately express that sentiment to the other. We never ask anyone attending one of our conferences to stand up before a group and make such a statement; we would never want to embarrass anyone. But often the results are reported to us anyway. Sometimes they are real tear-jerkers.

"Honey," said one fiftyish man engaging in this exercise, "I've never told you this, but I have always been impressed with the way you have decorated our home. It is so attractive, and I am really proud of your creativity." The wife was floored, completely flabbergasted. She had no idea that he had ever noticed anything hanging on the wall except the clean towel in the bathroom. He had rarely commented on any changes she had made in the house, and then only after she had asked for an opinion. In fact, she had entertained a sneaking suspicion for years that she could rearrange every stick of furniture except his favorite recliner, and he would never notice. And here he was, complimenting her creativity!

That was great, but it was also rather sad. Why hadn't he said something earlier? Surely some words of praise and appreciation would have been nice, especially in the years when she had spent large portions of each day in the house caring for their three children.

We have a responsibility to encourage. I will never forget the valentine Pearl gave me one year. It had a picture of Snoopy on the front, and these words: "Blockhead, I say some awful funny things sometimes, but I just want you to know I really love you and you're my Valentine." It was cute, I thought, but not the height of romance. Then I opened the card. Inside Pearl had written, "You are becoming more Christlike as the years go by." That brought tears to my eyes. Pearl thought she had laid an egg, giving me a funny valentine and I didn't even laugh. But the little comment she had included inside was such an encouragement in my Christian life that I was overwhelmed. She was so sensitive to my needs that she had touched exactly the right spot. She had graciously overlooked my many shortcomings and praised me beyond that which I deserved. She had focused solely on the positive.

Oh, how seldom do we dwell on the positives when communicating with our mate! Yet that is the lifeblood of encouragement. Usually we think about the garbage that didn't get taken out, the lawn that wasn't cut, the dishes that weren't done, the laundry that wasn't picked up at the cleaners, the gas tank that wasn't filled. We criticize each other when one of us is late, forgets to phone, burns the pot roast, or puts on a few pounds. We dwell on the negatives with our spouse (and our kids, too). But our responsibility is to demonstrate our love by encouraging and affirming. And may I remind you that it's too late at the funeral to bring flowers and make statements of praise and thankfulness? Start now—make the most of the time you have left together! Every day is a new opportunity to "say it positive" and "say it beautiful"!

EXALTING—BUILD 'EM UP!

We also have a *responsibility to exalt* those whom we love. Men, that means placing your wife above all else. That woman is more vital than anything in your life, except your relationship with the Lord. Make her feel like a queen! Think of her as supremely important. And ladies, do the same for your husband. There is nothing more gratifying to a man than to have his ego fed with honest expressions of genuine appreciation. We love to be loved, yes, but we need to feel valued.

As the old saying goes, there is no gain without pain. Sometimes exalting one's spouse entails sacrifice. The following story, although it doesn't concern a marriage relationship, illustrates my point well.

A few years ago, I was saddened to hear of the death of Gil Dodds, former track coach at Wheaton College. Dodds was a tremendous runner, for many years holding the world record for the indoor mile. He was one of my heroes, profoundly influencing my life through his example. One episode from his biography especially stands out.

The story is told of a major competition in which fifty thousand people looked on from the stands as Dodds entered the last lap of his event. His time was superb. Not only would he win the race, but a new world's record seemed easily within his grasp. Then a competitor in the next lane tripped and fell down. Gil Dodds felt a responsibility for that other young runner. He stopped, helped his competitor up, briefly made sure he was uninjured, then continued the race. Can you believe that Dodds still won? He did, but with that momentary hesitation, he had surrendered the world's record. How supremely unselfish he had been! He had placed the welfare of that other young man above his own transient glory, and had rendered himself worthy of far greater honor in the process.

Let me speak chiefly to the husbands here. Men, if you love your wife, your responsibility is to exalt her. She is much more than a mere acquaintance, an opposing runner in the next lane. She is running alongside you—for life. It's only fair to warn you that exalting her will probably cost you. It might mean the loss of a business contract, as you refuse to make seventy-hour work weeks a habit. It might mean that your golf score never sinks below the nineties because you can't play twice each weekend; you're spending time with the wife and kids instead. But the woman you married is more significant than any fleeting, earthly success. When you make it to heaven, it won't matter how many putts you made or how many deals you closed, if you've neglected your family in the meantime.

"So I can't have any hobbies? You're asking too much!" exclaimed a friend to me one day. That is not what I am suggesting. Rather, just be sure that your vocation and avocations don't interfere with home life. It's that simple. To paraphrase what a sports commentator recently said of Dallas Cowboys head coach and committed Christian, Tom Landry, "I know Tom, and there are more important things in his life than football." We should all be able to make similar statements about work, golf, racquetball, fishing, hunting, and jogging!

And ladies, if I may, let me just point out that the shoe fits your foot, too. Please don't let church and committee work, tennis clubs, Bible studies, careers, or children shove your husband into third or fourth place in your life. Your responsibility is to exalt and honor him, as well. When your spouse becomes a priority in your life—second to no one except the Lord—you'll reap great benefits. Believe me, I know.

Giving Pearl the position in my life that she deserves has been a problem for me over the years. Especially in my younger days, running, racquetball, snow-skiing, mountain climbing, camping, and teaching, all interfered with my time with my wife. I've had to cut back on my teaching schedule, delegate the planning and operation of our ministry's camps to others on our staff, and curtail some of my outdoor activities. The results—a deeper, richer relationship with Pearl, more meaningful ties with my kids—have been more than worth it.

ENDURING—A COMMITMENT TO CARE FOREVER

Finally, we have a *responsibility to endure* in a love relationship. As others have pointed out, we are to leave, leave not, and love. Genesis 2:24 states that "a man will leave his father and mother and be united to his wife, and they will become one flesh" (NIV). That's the leaving which is involved. Marriage entails a separation from former loyalties and a cleaving together. We still love our parents, brothers, sisters, and friends, but after the wedding day, our spouse becomes number one.

We then must leave not. In the words of Paul in 1 Corinthians 7:10-11, "To the married I give this command (not I, but the Lord): A wife must not separate from her husband. But if she does, she must remain unmarried or else be reconciled to her husband. And a husband must not divorce his wife" (NIV). Marriage is forever. Divorce is not an option for the Christian. If we are serious about our marriage, we'll be able to say to our husband or wife the same words which the Lord spoke to the Israelites in Isaiah 46:4, "Even to your old age, I shall be the same, And even to your graying years I shall bear you!" (NASB).

And of course, we must love. The command in Colossians 3:19 is: "Husbands, love your wives, and do not be embittered against them" (NASB; see also Ephesians 5:25).

And it is in Titus 2:4 that older women are exhorted to "train the younger women to love their husbands and children" (NIV). Responsibility is the initial ingredient in such love. It is what made Ruth leave her family and her friends and care for her mother-in-law in the lady's old age. It cannot be delegated; it must be embraced wholeheartedly.

THE SECOND INGREDIENT: RESPECT

If the story of Naomi and Ruth tells us something about the nature of love, the account of Ruth and Boaz reveals even more. As essential as responsibility is in a loving relationship, so also is respect.

Let's pick up the story in Ruth 2. Ruth and Naomi arrived in Bethlehem as the barley harvest was beginning (1:22). Shelter was found, but they faced a problem: they had nothing to eat. Ruth decided to glean in the fields, working behind the harvesters to gather what leftovers she could so that they might have food. She found herself in the field of a man named Boaz, who happened to be a relative of Naomi (2:1-3).

When Boaz spied the young woman at work, he inquired as to her identity. Upon learning that this was the girl who had so assisted his relative, Boaz was clearly impressed . . . and more than a little interested (2:5-6). He spoke to Ruth warmly:

> My daughter, listen to me. Don't go and glean in another field and don't go away from here. Stay here with my servant girls. Watch the field where the men are harvesting, and follow along after the girls. I have told the men not to touch you. And whenever you are thirsty, go and get a drink from the water jars the men have filled (Ruth 2:8-9 NIV).

In response, Ruth bowed before him, her face to the ground, treating him with reverence and honor (2:10). Why had she found such favor in his eyes? Boaz's grateful reply came quickly:

I've been told all about what you have done for your
mother-in-law since the death of your husband—how
you left your father and mother and your homeland
and came to live with a people you did not know
before. May the LORD repay you for what you have
done. May you be richly rewarded by the LORD, the
God of Israel, under whose wings you have come to
take refuge (Ruth 2:11-12 NIV).

The quality of Ruth's character riveted the attention of
Boaz, and with what tremendous respect did he treat her!
Bowled over by this young lady, he commanded his men to
leave her alone. (In other words, he had staked his claim.)
He praised her loyalty, integrity, and courage. As Ruth 2:14
further reveals, at mealtime, he even served her! He then
instructed his servants to treat her with deference, com-
manding that they pull out stalks of grain for her to gather,
making her work easier (2:15-16).

His was the same sort of esteem which Jacob accorded
Rachel. Genesis 29 tells us that Jacob served his father-in-
law for seven years in order to marry Rachel. Yet these
seven years seemed but as "a few days because of his love
for her" (29:20 NASB). He truly treasured her. No price is too
great to pay when love is present. Giving the best we have
to the one we love the most is an experience of utter ecstasy.

NOT ON MY LEVEL!

Unfortunately, it is true that we men often—consciously
or unconsciously—forget to give our best to our wife. Priorities press, and we allow ourselves to be trapped by the
tyranny of the urgent . . . and let that which is closest fall
into neglect. We disregard the fact that our wife is our
helpmate. We treat her as a second-class citizen, rather
than as an equal. But the apostle Peter teaches each man
that he must grant his wife "honor as a fellow-heir of the
grace of life" (1 Peter 3:7 NASB). Otherwise, his very prayers
will be hindered! It's that important.

Too few husbands see it that way. One man told me,

"The big problem in our marriage is that my wife has not developed as I have. She can't communicate on my level. She is awkward in social situations and doesn't fit in with my crowd." Not only did the man fail to regard his wife highly, he was actually embarrassed by her. I thought his remarks showed a blatant lack of understanding.

Didn't he realize, I asked, that his wife spent hours upon hours in the company of toddlers and preschoolers? Had he ever taken the time to help her develop the so-called social graces necessary to fit in with his "crowd"? Did he praise her both privately and publicly, even in front of the folks he was hung up on impressing? What had he done to build up her confidence, to show her that he valued her? The answer was easy. He had done nothing; he was the problem with their marriage.

Another item of knowledge which is essential if we men are to adequately respect our wife is that we must realize that we are not complete without her. That's right! In Eden, the Lord said, "It is not good for the man to be alone; I will make him a helper suitable for him" (Genesis 2:18 NASB). Eve was created because Adam needed her. She was essential—designed so that with her, he might be complete.

So it is absolutely necessary that we husbands respect our wives, that we value their opinions, that we view them—as Tim Timmons suggests in *Maximum Marriage*—as our completers, not our competitors (Timmons 1976, 27). And wives must feel the same way about their men. Centuries ago in a field in Bethlehem, Boaz demonstrated his esteem for Ruth by serving her; he provided for her; he honored her. Don't you know that she felt good? I would venture to say that Ruth must have felt absolutely terrific about herself. It must have been fairly easy for her to take the advice which Naomi was soon to offer.

THE THIRD INGREDIENT: RELATIONSHIP

With the respect that Boaz had shown the young woman, it was natural that a vital, loving, abiding relationship would develop between them—not the sort of temporary hook-up so common today. Having that kind of lasting relationship is an integral part of moving beyond just being in love. It is necessary if the love is to endure and the marriage is to prosper.

When Naomi heard of the kindness with which Boaz had treated Ruth, she instructed her daughter-in-law to slip on her most attractive outfit, spray on her most exotic perfume, and walk to the place where Boaz would be supervising the threshing of his harvested grain (3:3). Ruth was not to make her presence known until Boaz had finished eating and drinking. "When he lies down," said Naomi, "note the place where he is lying. Then go and uncover his feet and lie down. He will tell you what to do" (Ruth 3:4 NIV).

Ruth obeyed. Her actions may have been bold, but they were not brazen. And in the middle of the night, Boaz awoke to find a woman at his toes! Scripture records their conversation:

> "Who are you?" he asked.
> "I am your servant Ruth," she said. "Spread the corner of your garment over me, since you are a kinsman-redeemer."
> "The LORD bless you, my daughter," he replied. "This kindness is greater than that which you showed earlier: You have not run after the younger men, whether rich or poor. And now, my daughter, don't be afraid. I will do for you all you ask. All my fellow townsmen know that you are a woman of noble character" (Ruth 3:9-11 NIV).

Boaz looked at her, commended her as a woman of excellence, and promised to do what she had asked. We sense that a beautiful relationship was deepening between them. He had admired her loyalty and spirit, and her faithfulness in caring for Naomi. She trusted him enough to come to him in the middle of the night without fear; his character had already elicited her confidence in him. He did not take advantage of the situation either; this was not the moment for the physical. There would be time enough later, if indeed they were to be married.

And marriage was on Ruth's mind and heart. As Naomi's relative, Boaz was qualified as a kinsman-redeemer. He could consent to take the young woman as his wife. According to custom, the firstborn son of that union would be technically considered the child of Mahlon, Ruth's late husband. Thus, the line of Mahlon would be preserved.

Evidently, marriage was on the mind and heart of Boaz also. He was overjoyed that Ruth had approached him, rather than chasing after a younger man (3:10). What a priceless treasure this Moabitess was! Boaz was more than willing to marry her—but there was an obstacle which had to be overcome first.

"Although it is true that I am near of kin," said Boaz to Ruth, "there is a kinsman-redeemer nearer than I." He continued with these instructions, "Stay here for the night, and in the morning if he wants to redeem, good; let him redeem. But if he is not willing, as surely as the LORD lives I will do it" (Ruth 3:13 NIV).

THE FOURTH INGREDIENT: REDEMPTION

Boaz was willing to redeem Ruth. For all practical purposes, he held the key of her entrance into the nation of Israel. If she were to become one of God's chosen people, she'd be brought under the blessings of the Abrahamic covenant, which involved a seed and a land (see Genesis 12:1-3). As the fourth chapter of the book of Ruth shows, Boaz was able to open the door for her. Early the next morning, after seeing that Ruth left the threshing floor undetected, her good reputation intact, Boaz went to the town gate and sat there. He waited for the man who was Naomi's closest relative (4:1). The fellow walked by, and Boaz called out to him (4:2). Along with ten of the elders of the city, the two sat down. Then, said Boaz to the kinsman-redeemer:

Naomi, who has come back from Moab, is selling the piece of land that belonged to our brother Elimelech. I thought I should bring the matter to your attention and suggest that you buy it in the presence of these seated here and in the presence of the elders of my people. If you will redeem it, do so. But if you will not, tell me, so I will know. For no one has the right to do it except you, and I am next in line (Ruth 4:3-4 NIV).

When he finished speaking, the other man replied, "I will redeem it" (4:4 NIV). The lump in Boaz's throat probably ballooned to the size of a tennis ball. I imagine he took a deep breath before he continued with these words:

On the day you buy the land from Naomi and from Ruth the Moabitess, you acquire the dead man's widow, in order to maintain the name of the dead with his property (Ruth 4:5 NIV).

But this the man could not (or would not) do. I'm sure Boaz heaved a sigh of relief when his relative said, "You redeem it yourself" (4:6). Now Ruth would be his!

Ruth 4:8 states that the other man removed his sandal and handed it to Boaz. His action was a formal acknowledgement, a method of legalizing the transaction before witnesses. Proudly Boaz announced to the elders and all who would hear:

Today you are witnesses that I have bought from Naomi all the property of Elimelech, Kilion and Mahlon. I have also acquired Ruth the Moabitess, Mahlon's widow, as my wife, in order to maintain the name of the dead with his property, so that his name will not disappear from among his family or from the town records. Today you are witnesses! (Ruth 4:9-10 NIV).

Surely he was bursting with joy! A lovely woman of proven character was to become his wife. Boaz came forward. He was willing to redeem Ruth, to assume the responsibility for her, to care for her, and to create opportunities for her to fulfill her God-given potential. And in that sense, are all husbands "redeemers" of their wives.

The need for redemption in a love relationship extends far beyond that, however. Do you know what happened to Ruth the Moabitess next? She had the privilege of mothering one of the children in the lineage of David—King David's grandfather, in fact. And from the line of David is descended Jesus Christ Himself! Ruth and Boaz are included in the genealogy of the Savior.

A REDEEMER FOR US ALL

It is Jesus Christ to whom we must ultimately look for redemption. Christ, who spilled His blood on Calvary so that all who believe might be saved, is our only source of salvation (see John 3:16; 14:6). And it is Christ who best enables married love to survive the marriage.

When I stand before a couple whom I have just pronounced husband and wife, I remind them of four principles before they turn and walk back down the aisle together. I feel strongly about this message—it is one which must be taken to heart.

Marriage involves a *commitment*, I tell the bride and groom; this is forever. It also involves *companionship*; you are complete now. Through the years, you are going to change into what you are to become; the *challenge* to both of you is to change so that you might effectively meet each other's needs. Finally, you must never forget the place of *Christ* in your marriage; your life together should be something like a triangle, with Christ at the top; the closer you both move toward Him, the closer you will become to each other.

That's true for all of us, isn't it? The more we learn of the Lord, the more we talk to Him, the more we read and apply His Word, the closer we walk with Him. We become more like His Son, the only perfect individual to set foot on the face of this earth. The more like Christ we are, the easier it will be to put our spouse first, to think of his or her needs and those of our children, before our own. The Savior will be reflected in our home, and it will be fantastic!

Before we can grow like Him, we have to come to know Him. We have to accept the unconditional affection for us which He demonstrated so tangibly by His willing death. Only then will the love which we display toward our husband or wife begin to mirror—ever so slightly—the immense love shown us by the Lord. Only then will we begin to give consistent evidence of the kind of love which . . .

. . . remains when everyone else is gone;

. . . kisses away the tears and brings healing and comfort;

. . . charges no price for its services;

. . . endures the storms of separation, setbacks, and sickness without falling apart;

. . . will sacrifice, serve, and stay when it has every reason to leave;

. . . smiles at adversity and is as unchangeable as the character of God.

As we contemplate Christ's own immeasurable regard for us, we would do well to remember that "greater love hath no man than this, that a man lay down his life for his friends" (John 15:13 KJV). That is exactly what He did. And truly knowing Him necessitates fully, unabashedly, unreservedly, accepting that. If you have never taken that step of faith, I urge you to do so. You'll miss so much if you continue to delay . . . and the consequences are everlasting.

2
Make Full My Joy

Philippians 2:1-5

The royal wedding of England's Prince Andrew and Sarah Ferguson excited the hearts and minds of Britons and people the world over. It didn't seem to matter that both bride and groom had had well-publicized love affairs in the past. Andrew and Sarah seemed so refreshingly alive and in love with each other that only the present was important. The world was caught up in the romance of the moment. Heady questions such as these replaced the usual topics in daily conversations: What would Fergie's dress look like? Would she wear her fiery red hair up or let it cascade down? Where would the newlyweds honeymoon? Did the Queen approve of the match?

Millions around the globe awakened in the wee hours of that July morning to witness the live telecast of the ceremony. The major commercial and cable networks thoroughly covered the extravaganza; one even devoted a full day's broadcast to the event. On most stations, interspersed between footage of the wedding itself, interviews with the dressmaker, the caterers, and the royal staff, and reruns of Prince Charles and Lady Diana's own nuptials, were comments by media personalities.

I remember the statement of one fellow in particular. He said something to the effect that from this day on, it would all be "downhill" for Prince Andrew. The wedding would be the highlight of that young man's life, the crowning glory of his youth. From then on, he would be perpetually in the shadow of his older brother, the future king of England. In *Camelot* terminology, this was Andrew's "one bright shining moment."

Whether or not Andrew will have a few other high points in his life, it is true that the wedding day is often the happiest time in the relationship of any couple. Much too frequently, everything afterward is "all downhill." Maybe the decline is gradual—the marriage simply loses steam as the years chug along. Or the disintegration might be more rapid, the vitality and energy escaping in the explosion of a series of crises.

Do all marriages deflate like this? What about the case of Ruth and Boaz? We know a great deal about the love and courtship of these two. We know very little about their marriage—only that a son was born to them: Obed, the grandfather of David. I sometimes wonder why the Lord didn't tell us more. Could it be that their marriage wasn't worth talking about? Perhaps. Maybe their love for each other diminished as time passed. Yet somehow I can't quite believe that their wedded life became the scene of a failure. As we saw from their courtship, the ingredients of responsibility, respect, relationship, and redemption were present in their union from the very start. The foundation of their love was rock solid.

But the elements can chip away at even rock-solid foundations. That's why people who have committed their life to Christ sometimes find themselves, if not on the verge of divorce, at least in the throes of dissatisfaction with their mate. We are living in an age when many marriages, even Christian ones, don't make it.

Why the Vows Are Broken

The results of a survey conducted of 3,009 women were published recently in a popular tabloid. Of the respondents polled, only half indicated that they would marry their husband again, if given a second chance. Similar and equally shocking results were reported in the November 11, 1986, issue of *Woman's Day* magazine. Even the most conservative analysis of the findings of these two surveys suggests sobering conclusions. Literally thousands of women are unhappy with their man—their heartthrob has become a heartburn! If the statistics are truly representative of our nation, and fifty percent of America's women feel that their marriage is a mistake, it's no wonder that our divorce rate continues to soar. As it is, approximately one in every two new unions will predictably dissolve sometime before "till death do us part."

Why is there so much discontent? Why do so many marriages flounder? Perhaps it's because the ingredients of love seen in the story of Ruth and Boaz are not there from the beginning. Maybe genuine commitment—to each other and to Christ—is lacking. Certainly societal and economic pressures exert an unhealthy influence on many relationships. No doubt there is a gap between our expectations of marriage . . . and its reality.

The results of the *Woman's Day* survey mentioned earlier are worthy of special notice. In the article entitled "How Many Choices Do Women Really Have?" Martha Weinman Lear records and analyzes the responses of the sixty thousand women who took part in the voluntary survey. The group included a mix of full-time homemakers, career women devoted to achieving professional success, and ladies holding down more mundane jobs simply to make ends meet. While the magazine's methods weren't classically scientific (for instance, the respondents were not randomly selected according to the demographic make-up of the United States), the conclusions are still fascinating. Here are a few of the replies pertinent to love and marriage.

> Of the sixty thousand women responding . . .
> 50% would marry the same man again;
> 38% would not marry the same man again;
> 12% aren't sure if they would marry the same man again;
> 53% feel like their husband's partner;
> 39% feel like their husband's housekeeper;
> 27% feel like their husband's mother;

41% think their husband does less than his fair share around the house;

46% believe most men aren't willing take on day-to-day care of the children;

73% say that men expect too much from their wife in the way of housework;

75% say that men expect too much from their wife in terms of child care.

I think these statistics are more than interesting. Granted, they appeared in a secular magazine, and therefore may not reflect the mind-set of Mrs. Average American Christian. Yet today when the divorce rate exceeds all reasonable expectations, they give us food for thought. It seems to me that many of the women responding to the *Woman's Day* survey vent cries for help. Whether working at an outside job or remaining at home with the kids, they scream for their husband to become more involved in the action on the homefront. They want a man who will "go the extra mile" for them, who will serve unselfishly and share wholeheartedly in the tasks of child-rearing, home-building, and memory-making.

"She'll walk all over me if I do that!" exclaimed a man who I had suggested might be more thoughtful of his wife. Yet God's ideal is for each partner in wedlock to serve the other. When a man is sacrificially involved in pleasing his wife, she will respond similarly, with gratitude and appreciation. Think of the possibilities—a world of unselfish servants who happen to be married to each other! Neither husband nor wife becomes a doormat to be trodden upon in that sort of a marriage. Rather, both parties make concessions out of consideration for the other. It's "we" not "me" that is all-important.

Sounds simple, doesn't it? Oh, but it's not, because most of the time we expect our mate to fulfill our desires. We come to marriage not so much open-hearted as open-handed, ready to take but not prepared to give. And yet giving is what it is all about.

MAKE FULL MY JOY

The apostle Paul, an unmarried man, has produced some words of incredible wisdom which can be applied to the marriage relationship. At the time of the writing of the Epistle to the Philippians, Paul was penned up in prison. His future was uncertain, his life hanging by the thinnest of threads. Under the inspiration of the Holy Spirit, he began a letter—potentially his last—to his much-loved church at Philippi. As I was reading his message one day, I came across a little phrase in the Greek text: "Make full my joy" (Philippians 2:2).

Make full my joy—how well that sums up the desires and dreams of each blushing bride and nervous groom. That brief phrase expresses the longings, hopes, aspirations, and expectations we bring to the marriage altar. We marry because we want to be made complete—we desire that our emotional, mental, and physical needs be fully met. The secret of a superlative marriage is that we must be willing to do that for each other: the husband satisfying the wife, the wife fulfilling the longings of her man. Ideally, the wholehearted response of every bride and groom to each other should be, "I want to make full your joy! Your slightest wish is my supreme desire." And from that determination should come the direction of the entire relationship.

How can we go about it? How do we practically live out the process of making the joy of our spouse complete? That's where a portion of Paul's letter to the Philippians comes in. From Philippians 2:1-5, I believe that we can see (in application) the *desires* for marriage, the *direction* of marriage, and the means of *developing* a successful marriage. While Paul is not speaking specifically to husbands and wives, his words offer a wealth of insight into that delicate balancing act we call wedded love.

THE DESIRES—PHILIPPIANS 2:1

The apostle begins Philippians 2 with this statement: "If therefore there is any encouragement in Christ, if there is any consolation of love, if there is any fellowship of the Spirit, if any affection and compassion . . ." (2:1 NASB). As we consider these words, let us not forget the terrible loneliness which engulfed Paul in his prison cell. After he became a Christian, his whole life was consumed with taking Christ's message to the people. Now confined, he wasn't able to travel to his Bible classes and churches, and this lack of human contact distressed him because he loved to be around other Christians. In the very midst of his forced isolation, he cried out in despair—making an extremely personal statement, letting his readers know of four heartfelt desires he wished for them.

What were these desires? First of all, Paul longed for the Christians at Philippi to provide *encouragement* to one another. He also longed for them to practice the "consolation of love": the pure and simple expression of enduring devotion. He wanted them to continually convey their *love* to one another. He furthermore exhorted them to enjoy the *fellowship* of other Christians, made rich because of the Spirit of God in the lives of believers. Finally, Paul desired to see "affection and compassion" evident in the lives of the Philippians. Combined, I believe, these indicate his wish that they would *understand* one another.

Encouragement, love, fellowship, understanding—these are what Paul begged his fellow Christians in Philippi to spread among themselves (Philippians 2:1). They are also the basic reasons why men and women marry; they are what Pearl and I hoped to receive from each other as we stood before the minister and repeated our wedding vows. Yet as husbands and wives, we should not be as much concerned with being encouraged as with being encouraging, with being loved as with being loving, with being understood as with being understanding. In other words, we must focus on fulfilling the needs of our mate in these areas—making full the joy!

Let's look at the four desires of marriage more closely. How can we supply our spouse with encouragement, love, fellowship, and understanding? Here are a few ideas, and it's only fair to warn you men that I'll be picking on you again. The responsibility for creating a happy home rests on both the man and the woman to an extent but, as we discussed earlier, it is a burden which the husband, as the head of the house, must ultimately bear.

ENCOURAGEMENT

Paul, languishing in the Roman jail, exhorted the Philippians to provide one another with companionship and reassurance. Husbands and wives should encourage each other as well, but how difficult it is for us to consistently do so! Men, the apostle's message hits us right where we live. Women are basically responders. What they receive affects what they give. In fact, I have a theory that most women are what they are because of the man they live with. Does that sound simplistic? Think of it this way. If a wife lives with criticism or disapproval, she will become insecure; if her husband dishes out unkindness, she may become bitter or defiant; if he is indifferent, she will probably become cool and uncaring herself, or perhaps she will nag, nag, nag, simply to get his attention.

So what can we men do? We must be careful not to be negative with our wife. We can't exclude her from our life by becoming indifferent or by ignoring her. We must give honest compliments, frequent praise. We must show sin-·cere appreciation. This means recognizing her abilities and talents. It means thanking her for dinner, noticing (and mentioning) how tenderly she cares for the kids, showing gratitude for the extra money she earns or expressing thanks for the fact that she may have given up her career to raise the family. With genuine encouragement like that, a woman feels valued and honored. And she will respond in kind.

"Think of your wife as a computer," I told a man during a counseling situation. "Then, think of yourself as the programmer; what you put in is what you'll get out. If you pour loving affection, quality and quantity time into your relationship, your wife will return these. If you continue to give her short shrift . . . well, as one expert said when explaining why computers malfunction: 'Garbage in, garbage out.' That will probably describe your marriage." There is nothing more pathetic than a relationship which is decaying because of neglect.

LOVE

Not only did the imprisoned apostle Paul remind his readers of the value of encouragement, but he also eagerly advocated the "consolation of love." He wanted the Philippians to assure one another of their affection. There is tremendous comfort to be had in knowing that someone else cares deeply. Such knowledge is important in any close relationship—and it is vital in a marriage.

Now, maybe that seems obvious. Of course husbands and wives love each other! Why else would they have married? Yet women particularly need to be reminded that they are loved. It's a matter of security—how traumatic it is for a wife to feel that the foundation is shaky, that the man she married no longer cares for her.

The romance in marriage should continue long after the wedding day. Men, how long has it been since you told your wife that you literally adore her? Was "I love you" just a declaration that you made once long ago, as a twenty-year-old kid in a rented tuxedo? Do you only verbalize your affection in the bedroom? Are squeezes of the hand, tender kisses, gentle touches, simply precursors to sex, or are they a regular part of your time with your wife?

And what about anniversaries and birthdays? (I have found most men remember Christmas on their own!) What was the last present you gave your wife? How romantic was it? How personal? Was it electrifying . . . or just an electric appliance? Did your secretary pick it out, or did you take the time to select it yourself?

A thoughtful gift doesn't necessarily have to be jewelry, clothes, furs, or perfume, either. One of the nicest presents a friend of ours ever received from her husband was a set of insulated camouflage coveralls. I know what you're thinking! Yet this lady really enjoyed hunting, and her husband's gift was his way of saying, "Honey, you can come on up in my duck blind any time!" What meant the most to her was that he had taken the time to think of something that she would genuinely like.

Naturally, remembering special occasions isn't the only way that you can tangibly show your wife that you love her. There are always the "little things." Through the years, I've become sort of an expert on the little things, and one of my discoveries has been that the little things don't have to cost a lot. The city where we live is known as the "rose capital" of Texas. When we first moved to Tyler, I practically overwhelmed Pearl with flowers. And it didn't even hurt, because it was so inexpensive to do so.

One evening in particular, I remember driving home from Dallas and stopping at a roadside restaurant for a box of Pearl's favorite peanut brittle (it was all of forty-nine cents). Then as I hit the outskirts of Tyler, I stopped at a rose stand and splurged some more—I forked over twenty-five cents for a dozen miniature red roses. Into the house I strode, and for less than dollar, I gave my wife flowers and candy! Now Pearl is not a slow study; she knew that I hadn't spent a week's paycheck to make her happy. But she was pleased nonetheless, because I had showed her in a concrete way that I appreciated and loved her.

Maybe roses are expensive in your home town. Try daisies! Or walk around the side of the house and pick a flower off the bush. Bring it in to your wife and see what she does. It's a little thing, but it tells her, "I love you." And she is practically guaranteed to respond favorably to your consistent show of affection and constant assurance of security.

FELLOWSHIP

What else did Paul longingly exhort the Philippians to practice while he was in prison? He reminded them of the importance of fellowship with other Christians—that wonderful bond which the Spirit enables us to have with one another. Such fellowship involves heart-to-heart communication, an ingredient essential in any good marriage as well.

Fellows, your wife wants a companion who will share of himself. She wants to know what happened at work, what problems cropped up, what successes were achieved. She wants a prayer partner who is truly a spiritual leader in the home. And she wants a good listener who is interested in what she has to say.

Most men don't realize that their fellowship with their wife is much like their fellowship with God. God wants us to speak with Him, to consult Him, to listen to Him. And as we communicate with Him, we'll become better able to communicate with our spouse. Many men have told me that the key to their becoming open and vulnerable with their wife is that they've begun to be that way with the Lord, first. Then He enables it to happen.

May I make a suggestion? Men, why not today begin praying with your wife? It is perhaps the best way to start developing a close fellowship with her. As you pray together, you'll draw closer to each other and to the Lord. Another of Ruth Harms Calkin's poems expresses it so well. This is what she has to say about the "Cementing Force" of prayer between a husband and a wife:

> The newly married couple asked:
> "What is the greatest cementing force
> In all your years of marriage?"
> Lord, there are many cementing forces:
> Little things, big things
> Enormously big things!
> But when we sum it all up
> The one changeless pattern is this:
> *We have prayed for* each other
> And *with* each other
> Through all the cumulative years.
> Problems? Yes, but we've prayed.
> Misunderstanding? Confusion?
> Yes, but we've prayed.
> Goals? Laughter? Joy? Delight?

Yes, and we've prayed.
We've prayed under rain-filled clouds
And at the top of our private hill.
We've prayed on a sandy beach
With foam covering our feet
And the wind kissing our faces.
We've prayed in the tangle of traffic
And in the still blue twilight.
We've laughed and prayed
Wept and prayed
We've held each other and prayed.
We've prayed about budgets and bills
About victories and defeats
About neighbors and friends
About missions and milestones.
Lord, does it begin to sound
As though all our life together
Has been one long prayer?
Perhaps in a way it has!
Could that be the reason
Why all our life together
Seems one long joy?

UNDERSTANDING

The fourth desire expressed by the jailed apostle Paul
was that of understanding, as he called for "affection and
compassion." The word "affection" may also be rendered
"tenderheartedness." Paul urged his brothers and sisters in
Christ to be sensitive to what each was going through. He
prayed that the Philippians would be compassionately and
constructively involved with one another.

When we marry, we expect our partner to empathize
with us, to be actively involved with us, and to be willing
and able to understand us. We strongly desire our spouse to
be sensitive to our hopes, fears, dreams, and needs. But
what a tremendous challenge to us all are these words of
St. Francis of Assisi: "Lord, grant that I may seek more to
understand than to be understood." That must be our aim.

When we become frustrated, bitter, angry, or resentful because our mate doesn't understand us, our marriage becomes stuck in a holding pattern. Like a plane circling the airport, we go nowhere. The right response is to switch frequencies and try to understand.

As Pearl will tell you, I can be a difficult person to live with. More than once through the years my wife has felt misunderstood. She had resigned herself to coping with my selfish, egotistic need to always be right . . . until the day I brought home a surprise gift for her. It was a fancy new iron—computerized, loaded with extra features. It would beep when left on too long, then it would turn itself off. It had a setting for every fabric the world has ever known. It was a marvel of modern technology which any woman would be proud to own . . . except Pearl. She hated it.

When I saw her lack of appreciation, I became angry. How ungrateful she was! But then the Lord laid bare my motives and caused me to see myself in a light I didn't like. Pearl wasn't being selfish in rejecting my gift. Her attitude was a response to the fact that I hadn't even attempted to understand what her ideas were on the matter. All she wanted was a simple, functional iron. And she would be the one using it, after all! Consultation, communication, and caring on my part could have avoided a confrontation. A little understanding would have spared us a barrage of angry words (and would have saved me quite a bit of money, too).

THE DIRECTION—PHILIPPIANS 2:2

We marry for certain reasons. We crave encouragement, love, fellowship, and understanding—the things Paul spoke of while confined in the Roman jail. As he continues his letter to the church at Philippi, the apostle adds this fourfold exhortation: "Make my joy complete by being of the same mind, maintaining the same love, united in spirit, intent on one purpose" (2:2 NASB). His wishes for the Philippian believers are also gems of wisdom to those of us who are married.

Specifically, Paul mentions four goals which can apply to marriage. As we strive to fulfill the desires of our mate, these are the directions into which our marriage ought to be heading. We should work toward becoming:

1. Of the same mind,
2. Of the same love,
3. Of the same spirit,
4. Of the same purpose.

OF THE SAME MIND

Paul urged his readers to be "of the same mind." What is that "same mind"? It is the mind of Christ. That means that as husbands and wives, we must seek to be more concerned about the will of God and the thoughts of Christ than we are about the rightness of our own opinions. We must be open to the fact that we are not infallible, that we are not always right, that other viewpoints are possible. Such openmindedness leaves the door ajar for Christ to work in a relationship. He is able to function as the great arbiter of any and all human disagreement.

Why did Paul plead for the Christians at Philippi to be likeminded? It was because the situation there was not too pleasant. As Philippians 4:2-3 reveals, two ladies named Euodia and Syntyche (I like to think of them as the president of the women's association and the soprano in the choir) were fussing and feuding. Their battles were dividing the church. Apparently neither one of them was willing to bend. And thus neither of them could possibly have been open to the direction and leading of the Lord.

At least Euodia and Syntyche didn't have to live together under the same roof. How much worse when such stubborn conduct characterizes a marriage! It invites disaster. Conflict demands compromise, cooperation, and consideration.

How are these achieved? Let's consider an example from the Bible as we look at a scene from the life of Jacob. Jacob had not one, but two wives to think about. He had to strive to be of the same mind with two women—a nearly impossible task and one at which he often failed. No wonder the Bible doesn't sanction polygamy! But one particular episode in Jacob's married life is a beautiful example of husbands and wives working together to be of one mind.

Jacob had lived in the land of his father-in-law, Laban, for twenty years when the Lord commanded him, "Return to the land of your fathers and to your relatives, and I will be with you" (Genesis 31:3 NASB). The circumstances had deteriorated; Laban and his sons were far less friendly than before. The word of the Lord came to Jacob with instructions to go. What did Jacob do then? Scripture tells us that he went out into the field and consulted his wives, Rachel and Leah, about his decision to leave. The women agreed—their acquiescence verifying God's command. And so, with complete likemindedness, they left the land of Paddan-aram and returned to Canaan. The women were leaving their homeland, their relatives, everything they had known since birth. Potentially such a departure could have caused bitterness and resentment, but the individuals involved had sought the will of God in the matter; they were of one mind.

Pearl and I made a commitment early in our marriage that we would be of one mind—in total agreement—before we would make any major decisions or changes. I wasn't going to holler the word "Submit!" at her, while sticking a Bible turned to 1 Peter 3:1 under her nose, whenever I wanted my way. And she wasn't going to scratch, pick, and peck at me to make me give in on an issue. In short, long ago we agreed to agree agreeably before taking important steps!

Of course we've had to compromise and cooperate with each other. In one area of our lives this has been especially true of late. For the past few years now, I have had a strong desire to live in one of the recreational communities where I minister. It would be wonderful to my way of thinking to have golf, tennis, swimming, and unlimited jogging routes available. Pearl, on the other hand, believes that a woman's place is in the mall. I haven't been able to convince her of the tremendous "spiritual benefits" she'd get from spending forty-five minutes driving into town to shop. So, we still live in the city. . . close to the mall. And we agree that until we are of one mind on the matter, we are not going to move.

BUT, WHAT IF. . . ?

"That's okay for you to say," rejoined a young woman after one of my classes one day. "My husband is not a Christian! We can't seem to agree on much of anything: where the kids should attend school, what church activities they'll be permitted to participate in, whether or not we'll buy a larger house, even whose family we'll visit for the holidays. It is hard to be of the same mind!"

And she is tragically right. Only two Christians can truly be likeminded in the manner meant by Paul. It is impossible to have the mind of Christ if we do not know Him personally as Lord and Savior. That is why the apostle further teaches us in 2 Corinthians 6:14, "Do not be bound together with unbelievers; for what partnership have righteousness and lawlessness, or what fellowship has light with darkness?" (NASB).

What if you are yoked with an unbeliever? What are your alternatives as you seek to turn your marriage into the direction God would have it to go? Should you divorce your spouse? No, although it may be very difficult, determine to stay married. Should you try to win your mate to Christ? Yes, but ramming Scripture down his or her throat isn't the way to go about it. Don't self-righteously stomp off to church every Sunday morning and Wednesday evening, either. I'm not saying don't go, but try not to make a big production of your "holiness."

What can you do? Pray. Pray long and hard for your husband or wife, and for your children. Enlist a few trusted, *close-mouthed* friends to pray as well. The heart of every believer should ache with you . . . but even with the plague of complacency infecting the Christian community, remember that God knows, understands, and cares. Pray for yourself, that the Lord would grant you patience and would transform you into His image. Pray that He would make you into a living, walking, breathing, beautiful testimony to His power, graciousness, and love. How you live will do more to win your loved one to Christ than what you say—it's *life* over *lip!* Remember also to read God's Word for growth and comfort. And then leave the results to Him. God Himself touched your life and brought you to a saving knowledge of His Son; He can do the same for that man or woman to whom you are married. Ultimately, only the Lord can turn the hearts of two into the direction of the One.

OF THE SAME LOVE

Paul continued his message to the divided church at Philippi by beseeching his readers to maintain "the same love." What kind of love is that? It is *agape* love—the love of Christ. It is the love which prompted the Creator of all things to wash the feet of His disciples. It is the unconditional, self-sacrificing love which carried Jesus Christ to the cross, and to the ultimate sacrifice awaiting Him there. Men and women can comprehend nothing of that sort of love until they come to know God through His Son. Then they begin to truly understand what agape love is all about.

God desires that the affections of husbands and wives be aimed in the direction of achieving agape love. Husbands are commanded in Ephesians 5 to steer that course in the relationship. As Ephesians 5:25 puts it, "Husbands, love your wives, just as Christ loved the church and gave Himself up for her" (NASB). It's a tall order, but working toward such sameness of love has got to be an essential goal of Christian marriage. It means relinquishing "rights" in favor of serving the Savior by serving each other.

The relationship between John and Louis McCollum comes to mind here, for their life together embodied daily the principles of agape love. The McCollums resided at Hide-A-Way Lake for years and attended our church there regularly. This vibrant, warm couple was a pleasure to be around—so active and in love with each other!

While working in the yard one day, Louis tripped over a garden hose, breaking her hip. Thus started what seemed to be an endless round of hospital stays. John, in one of the most unselfish displays of loving concern I've ever seen, cared night and day for Louis: cooking, cleaning, carrying the load for two. Then came the day when John collapsed in exhaustion, and went home to be with the Lord. He had truly sacrificed everything for the woman he loved. He had given his very best, his last ounce of energy, for her.

OF THE SAME SPIRIT

As we strive for oneness of mind and of love in our marriage, we should also aim to become "united in spirit," as Paul exhorts the Philippians. That means letting the Spirit of God work in our lives to bear the fruit of "love, joy, peace, patience, kindness, goodness, faithfulness, gentleness, self control" mentioned in Galatians 5:22-23 (NASB).

Being of one spirit is rather like being of one mind, because it is essential that we focus on Christ in the process of becoming like-spirited. A verse which has been vital to Pearl and me since the days of our courtship is Isaiah 26:3, "Thou wilt keep him in perfect peace, whose mind is stayed on thee, because he trusteth in thee" (KJV). It is inscribed on the inside of my wedding band.

By keeping our minds upon Christ, and by desiring above all to please Him, Pearl and I have avoided many potholes in the road we've traveled together. We have been able to pray together for the will of God to be made evident. We have often—even independently—thought the same thoughts and prayed the same prayers. More often than not, we have come to the same conclusions and have been able to forge ahead with confidence.

At times, of course, we've had differences of opinion, but

the Spirit of God working in our lives has enabled us ultimately to settle our differences in peace and unity. That is
what it is to be of the same spirit.

OF THE SAME PURPOSE

And finally, Paul begged the Philippians to remain "intent on one purpose." What is that purpose? It is to please
God. When husbands and wives focus on pleasing the Lord
in and through their lives, then a whole lot of marital
problems fall by the wayside. As we unselfishly seek to
honor God in all that we say and do, disharmony can be
effectively disarmed!

So many times I have wanted things—material items,
responses from Pearl, changes in our home—for selfish
gratification. How revealing it is to explore and expose
ourselves to the question: Is it going to help me please God?
If we're honest, the answer will often be no. Will it please
God? Ask that of yourself before you make your next commitment. Sometimes even good things won't please Him if
other areas of our life suffer. I think of a young couple I
know who live in San Antonio, Texas. The husband was
recently asked to be a deacon in his church. A good thing,
right? That would please God for sure! But the young man
thoughtfully and prayerfully declined to serve for the present. He felt that his other obligations—work, involvement
in a businessmen's ministry, Sunday school teaching—were
taking away enough of his time from his wife and their
little one-year-old son. One more commitment, even a good
one, would not be honoring to God because it would take
precious time away from his family. My friend wisely said
no.

THE DEVELOPMENT—PHILIPPIANS 2:3-5

One mind, one love, one spirit, one purpose—these are
the directions toward which we should attempt to guide
our marriage. As the apostle Paul continues his message in
Philippians 2:3-5, he gives us five rules to grow by:

Do nothing from selfishness or empty conceit, but with humility of mind let each of you regard one another as more important than himself; do not merely look out for your own personal interests, but also for the interests of others. Have this attitude in yourselves which was also in Christ Jesus (NASB).

Paul's words suggest five regulations to follow as we develop our marriage in accordance with God's direction. They are guidelines to help us as we strive to become mentally, emotionally, physically, and spiritually united. Let's look at them briefly.

RULE 1: DO NOTHING FROM SELFISHNESS

The most selfish creatures I can think of are tiny babies. The little beings cry when wet, hungry, thirsty, colicky, hot, or cold. They voice their demands until they are diapered, fed, given medicine, put to bed, undressed, or dressed. They scream until the need is met.

Potentially the second most selfish creature alive is a demanding, immature husband. If he is oblivious to responsibilities around the home, selfish in his demands for sex, puffed up about his own importance, he is as much fun to have around as a screaming baby. And I'd have to place a selfish wife next in the line of immaturity. We must make a conscious effort to avoid self-seeking when interacting with our mate. The "I want what I want and I want it now!" mentality has sunk more than one marital ship.

RULE 2: DO NOTHING FROM EMPTY CONCEIT

Men and women, remember your spouse is a companion, not a competitor—and so your motives must be pure, your actions based on something other than "empty conceit." Realize that you don't have to win every argument just to protect your ego. Refuse to feel that you have got to be proved right, no matter what the cost. Accept the responsibility for mistakes you have made. Determine afresh to be approachable with your husband or wife and kids. And take the words "I told you so" out of your vocabulary.

RULE 3: BUT WITH HUMILITY OF MIND, REGARD ONE ANOTHER AS MORE IMPORTANT THAN YOURSELF

Try adopting an attitude of transparent humility. Tell your mate (and mean it), "Honey, I don't deserve someone as terrific as you." If necessary, ask God to convince you that it's true! You'll find it easier if you focus on the strengths of your spouse, not on his or her weaknesses.

RULE 4: DO NOT MERELY LOOK OUT FOR YOUR OWN INTERESTS, BUT ALSO FOR THE INTERESTS OF OTHERS

Think of it this way: when you're married, your possessions aren't only yours any longer. They belong to both of you. Remember that the next time she dents your pick-up or you melt the lid to her Tupperware bowl! You'll sidestep more than a few arguments.

Married couples must also remember the necessity of sharing plans and interests. Too much golf with the guys and bridge with the gals has the potential of ruining many an intimate moment. Don't forget that a little togetherness goes a long way in the making of a magical marriage.

RULE 5: LET THE ATTITUDE OF CHRIST BE IN YOU

In 2 Corinthians 10:5, Paul admits that he is "taking every thought captive to the obedience of Christ" (NASB). In every facet of life—with our wife, husband, kids, business associates, friends—it is our responsibility as a Christian to think like Jesus Christ and act in obedience to God's Word. Our obligation certainly continues after we walk in the door at home; in fact, it never ends. There is no "time-off" in the life of a committed believer for unChristlike behavior. We're sentenced to life with Him, and thank God that we are!

Marriage is an opportunity for us to grow. If there are

areas of conflict, trouble spots, sources of weakness, we won't solve them by attempting to change our spouse. We can only change ourself by allowing God to work in our life. And when we do become different, our mate will change in response. Marriage offers virtually limitless chances for personal growth—countless occasions in which we can exhibit the attitudes of Christ. It is a beautiful laboratory for development—and just because we are developing, doesn't mean that we should look on marriage as a darkroom experience! Rather, it is a vehicle through which God can work to conform us to the image of His Son (see 2 Corinthians 3:18).

FINAL THOUGHTS

God has marvelously moved in my own marriage. Over the years, He has given Pearl and me a sweeter and deeper relationship, as well as a better understanding of our children. The transformation has been slow, and it didn't really start until we were willing to submit to whatever the Lord wanted us to do and to be.

In 1972, we reached a pivotal point in our life together. One area of ministry had been shut off—our choices were for me to enter the business world or continue in another full-time ministry. We had to determine what God wanted—and it took a lot of prayer. Our choice to remain in full-time Christian service is not what everyone should select, but it is what the Lord wanted us to do. And Pearl and I bear witness to the fact that from the moment of our mutual decision onward, our needs began to be met.

I do not mean to suggest that our road has always been smooth, because it has contained its share of rough spots. We bear marks and scars, yes, but bumps are what you build on. Laying our foundation on the rock of Christ is what has kept our marriage house intact. Through the tough times especially, He has enabled our relationship to grow stronger, our affection to deepen.

God wanted us to stop worrying about our own problems—and to start looking at the world around which is dying without Jesus Christ. We prayed together for burning hearts, busy hands, and bloody feet—whatever it would take to spread the gospel. And God receives full credit for any small successes we may have had, because they have been His totally.

As we consider our marriage, men, the challenge to us is to sacrificially meet the needs and desires of our woman. She will respond to our determined commitment. Ladies, the opportunity is there for you to make life terrific for your husband. We must be willing to look beyond ourselves during the portion of eternity that we are on the earth.

Would you like a role model? That's easy. In the pages of Scripture itself is a candid portrait of a couple who managed to remain tremendously happy even after they were married. We're going to look at God's ideal of a loving, thriving, vibrant union as seen in Scripture, as we turn to the pages of the Song of Solomon. Read on.

Part Two

Making Full the Joy

3

Solomon's Greatest Love Song

It is sundown at Camelot. King Arthur walks alone on a terrace of his onstage castle. Spotlights illumine his form as the background dims in the red glow of the day's end. Arthur pauses, perplexed. He looks out upon the audience and then begins to haltingly sing these unforgettable words:

> How to handle a woman.
> There's a way, said a wise old man,
> A way known by every woman
> Since the whole rigamarole began.
> Do I flatter her? I begged him answer.
> Do I threaten, cajole or plead?
> Do I brood or play the gay romancer?
> Said he smiling, No indeed.
> How to handle a woman.
> Mark me well, I will tell you sir,
> The way to handle a woman is to love her,
> Simply love her, merely love her, love her, love her.
>
> (Alan Jay Lerner and Frederick Loewe)

That may be the theater . . . but what a wealth of truth there is in that song! How to handle a woman? Men—King Arthur's answer speaks to us all: love her, simply love her, merely love her . . . tenderly, consistently, prayerfully, sacrificially. Just how to do that is the theme of an entire book of the Old Testament: the Song of Solomon.

Some biblical scholars disagree with this sort of literal interpretation of the text. It has been argued that the Song of Solomon should be interpreted as a symbolic representation of the love of God for the nation Israel. Others have insisted that it is chiefly a portrait of Christ and His bride, the church. But I've found that the safest thing to do when examining Scripture is to take what is there literally. And taken literally, the Song is a glorification of wedded love.

SOLOMON'S GREATEST HIT

1 Kings 4:32 tells us of Solomon: "He spoke three thousand proverbs and his songs numbered a thousand and five" (NIV). Of these thousand and five, the Song of Solomon is the longest included in Scripture. It is what we might label the king's "greatest hit," his biblical "platinum record." As it is sometimes called, it is truly his Song of Songs.

What is it about? It is a piece which came straight from the heart of the king, a beautiful lyric which paints a vivid and evocative (and tastefully erotic) portrait of wedded love. Much of its language is figurative; some of it is difficult to understand, at least at first. Many of the images may seem obscure to us. But after careful consideration, the beauty of the words spoken by two lovers becomes crystal clear.

The principles of this account of a flesh-and-blood couple can and should be applied to our marriage. The book is filled with practical advice on the relationship between husband and wife.

But Solomon's Song, while primarily the story of a man and a woman, also offers us many tools for spiritual growth. Our marriage is the closest earthly parallel we know of to our relationship with the Lord. In fact, marriage is a training ground which prepares us for eternity, as we learn ultimately to live for one person alone: Jesus Christ. Turning from the charred remains of her own broken home, Patti Roberts so eloquently writes in *Ashes to Gold*:

The Christian marriage is meant to be a miniaturized, made-just-for-two, identical replica of Christ and His commitment to the Church. And that relationship— between Christ and His beloved—is the whole point of human history. Time is allowed to exist only so that the bride can be made fully ready, beautified, tried and proven worthy of the great price that was paid for her. Then time will cease and the Lover and the beloved will be joined together forever (Roberts 1983, 114-115).

While we wait for that moment of union, God can use the depiction of ideal human love that is the Song of Songs to touch our dead hearts, our distorted affections, our diseased wills . . . so that we might know more of His great love for us.

ABOUT THE AUTHOR

One wonders how Solomon could have penned such an intensely romantic love story, and then turned around later in his life and had "seven hundred wives of royal birth and three hundred concubines" (1 Kings 11:3 NIV). The Song of Songs was probably written before all of that, before Solomon dissipated his potential by surrendering his principles. The Song deals only with the relationship between the king· and his first bride, Shulamith. It is the poetic account of the time when he was young and in the raptures of first love, completely smitten with the country girl from Lebanon.

Solomon also wrote Ecclesiastes and Proverbs. When a man is young, he sings songs, as Solomon did in his great love ballad. The world seems an arena of unlimited opportunity to the fellow in his twenties and thirties. Then come some of the storms of life: problems in the workplace, rebellious kids, impossible schedules, sagging physique. Mid-life unexpectedly encroaches on what seemed to be a happy and productive youth, and when a man reaches his middle years, he often complains about the vanity of his existence. Everything he has worked so hard to achieve seems meaningless and purposeless. It is the time of the mid-life crisis, and this is the point in his life at which I believe Solomon—by then a flamboyant playboy—produced Ecclesiastes, a thousand women after his own first love. (For a more complete look at this idea, see my book *Ecclesiastes: The Mid-Life Crisis*, Loizeaux Brothers, 1987.)

When a man comes to the final years of his life—assuming the experience of living hasn't rendered him hopelessly bitter—he has the capacity to speak words of tremendous wisdom. That is the stage which I contend Solomon had reached when he wrote the book of Proverbs. He was nearing the end of his days and, along with his gray hairs, he had earned the right to write.

It is interesting that nowhere in Proverbs does Solomon recommend polygamy. He practiced it, in his lifetime taking for himself one thousand wives and concubines, but he never endorsed the idea of multiple marriages. Passages in Proverbs which pertain to marriage, such as Proverbs 5:18, 12:4, 18:22, and 19:14, speak of the relationship between one woman and one man. Perhaps in his later years, Solomon looked back wistfully at the springtime of his youth—when he had fallen head over heels for the dark and lovely maiden from the north.

THE LOVERS

Who was this young lady who captured the heart of a king? Let me fill you in on the background of the lovers. Following the tragic era recorded in the book of Judges, the Israelites clamored for a king. They were given Saul (1050-1010 B.C.), who eventually committed suicide on the field of battle. David (1010-970 B.C.) ascended to the throne next, and at his death was succeeded by Solomon (970-930 B.C.), his eldest surviving son by Bathsheba.

The kingdom reached its pinnacle under Solomon's leadership. It is an understatement to say that he was the wealthiest of all the kings. His possessions and landholdings would place him at the top of the list of the ten richest men anywhere and anytime. Among his vast properties were vineyards scattered across the country. One rather large tract was located at Baal-hamon, far up into the northern part of Galilee in the foothills of the mountains of Lebanon. For more reasons than one, it was a piece of real estate which Solomon never regretted purchasing.

While one day visiting the vineyard at Baal-hamon— which had been leased out to keepers who cared for it (8:11)—Solomon caught a glimpse of a suntanned young girl, working in the fields. She was lovely, with sparkling eyes, luxuriant black hair, and a firm, supple body. Her natural beauty sharply contrasted with the painted-on prettiness of the women who spent their days primping in the palace, hoping to be noticed by the king. This girl, Shulamith, was different . . . and Solomon was attracted back to Baal-hamon on many occasions. A fellow can always find an excuse to make a business trip when there is a little more in it for him than business!

Finally, Solomon got up enough nerve to ask Shulamith for her hand in marriage. Most girls would have thrown themselves at his feet—breathlessly giving their agreement as soon as the words were out of his mouth. Not Shulamith. She was a serious, level-headed thinker. Before she said yes, she considered the full implications of the decision she would be making. Marriage to Solomon would mean leaving her home and giving up her simple lifestyle for the cat-eat-cat world of the palace, where too many females would be crouched, ready to sink their claws into her man. She would be leaving the country for the capital—where she might feel insecure when faced with competition from the perfumed, painted, glittery, sophisticated ladies of the court. Not only that, but she would have to share her husband with a round-the-clock job which would take much of his time away from her and from which he could never retire.

THE STORY

What a joyous moment it was for Solomon when Shulamith finally accepted his proposal! As the Song of Solomon opens, we observe her first visit to Jerusalem and the palace (1:1–2:17). Later, we witness some anxious moments as the time of the wedding draws near. Then we encounter the magnificent picture of the wedding procession . . . and following, the tenderness of the wedding night (3:1–5:1). After a time, a problem arises in the marriage: Shulamith becomes indifferent to Solomon's sexual advances. But the challenge is met and the difficulty overcome (5:2–6:13). We see the account of another night, as the marriage has progressed in the physical realm. The book closes as the married lovers take a vacation, journeying once again to Shulamith's homeland, Lebanon, where their love first blossomed (7:1–8:14).

In such manner does Scripture give us little scenes from their diary of love—capsules of significant events in the relationship between the king and the country girl. As we study, we will break the account into the following episodes:

Courtship—Song of Solomon 1:1–2:17
Commitment—Song of Solomon 3:1–5:1
Challenge—Song of Solomon 5:2–6:13
Communion—Song of Solomon 7:1–8:14

We'll be looking at the text on a verse-by-verse basis, using S. Craig Glickman's insightful translation found in his book, *A Song for Lovers* (InterVarsity Press 1976, 153-170). By considering God's Word as it is written, we'll discover how effectively and completely Scripture can minister to our needs.

CHANGES

The Song of Solomon has a great deal to say to us as Christian husbands and wives. It has literally transformed my attitudes about the physical relationship between a woman and a man. In many places, the Word of God speaks boldly about the consequences of sexual sins and sexual disobedience. Is it not logical that the Holy Spirit would give us guidelines for sexual obedience—insights into the proper development of the physical relationship within a marriage? I trust that by studying Solomon's song of love, you'll recognize some areas in your married life where you may have some adjustments to make.

In my experiences as a pastor and counselor, I've seen that there can be grave misunderstanding between Christian husbands and wives concerning the place of the physical in their marriage. Certainly part of this may be blamed on the influence of our culture.

A pervasive attitude in our society today is that the wife ought to burst into some sort of flaming torch of desire the second her husband walks in the door. If she fails to aggressively initiate the lovemaking at home, he will satisfy himself elsewhere—at the club, the office, the convention. The basic problem with the flaming torch theory is that when Mr. Average Husband steps into his house at six o'clock each evening, it is only after Mrs. Average Wife has spent the day dealing with three kids, two carpools, and at least one committee meeting—assuming she hasn't worked at a full-time job outside the home herself. She's washed a load of clothes (probably including her husband's dirty socks—no thrill, according to my wife), emptied the wastebaskets, prepared the evening meal, and changed a dozen diapers. What she'd really like to do is collapse onto the bed . . . and sleep.

Many a man is simply insensitive to the fatigue and time pressure which are typical of the life of his wife. As we discussed in a previous chapter, it's easy for a fellow to come home, settle down with the paper till dinner, and then watch television (on a full stomach, of course) until bedtime. How could a wife, who has had to fly solo all evening in getting the dishes done and the kids in bed, become a nuclear reactor later on in the bedroom? It's virtually impossible!

TROUBLE SPOTS

Exhaustion isn't the only reason why husbands and wives sometimes have difficulty in the physical area of their marriage. What else can cause problems? Here are some observations and reflections.

1. Some attitudes toward sex in marriage are holdovers from the Victorian era. The idea that lovemaking was designed by God solely for propagation and not for pleasure is wrong, as we'll observe from the Song of Solomon. Yet many women whom I've counseled see it this way. To them, the physical is something to be endured, a duty; it is not something to be enjoyed. This outlook can naturally cause problems in a couple's intimacy.

2. Another frequent trouble spot in a couple's physical relationship is that too many men forget that women are essentially responders. And they cannot respond honestly and enthusiastically to their husband's caresses if they are bitter or resentful because of unresolved conflicts in the marriage. Many men operate on the theory that marital problems can be patched up by a session of lovemaking. In reality, the conflict is only submerged when that takes place. It smolders for a later explosion, and the wife feels used. The relationship is affected. As we'll discover in the Song of Solomon, conflicts must be solved outside the bedroom in order for the physical relationship to be all that God intends it to be.

3. A woman's desire for the physical builds more slowly that a man's. There are biological and emotional differences between the sexes which have been well documented by physicians and psychologists. I heartily recommend Dr. James Dobson's *What Wives Wish Their Husbands Knew About Women* (Tyndale, 1975) to any reader wanting a more thorough understanding of the subject. My point is that a woman needs to be prepared for lovemaking. It cannot be just a momentary encounter, if it is to be fulfilling! This we will learn also from reading of Solomon and Shulamith.

PRINCIPLES

As we examine how the king and his bride overcome certain obstacles in their journey toward intimacy, it is my hope that we will come away convinced of at least two biblical principles concerning the physical relationship between a man and wife.

Principle 1: Let's recognize that the expression of love involves more than the experience of love. True lovemaking calls for candid conversation—the honest expression of emotion. Solomon talks to his bride and she to him. Speaking in love, focusing on the positive attributes of each other, sharing personal longings—these forms of communication are all vital parts of intimacy.

Principle 2: Within marriage, the physical relationship is innately pure and holy and lovely. It is not evil. It should not provoke guilt. When handled properly, sex is a gift of incredible beauty from God to His children.

FOUR PLANES

As we watch the budding and progression of Solomon and Shulamith's love for each other, we will also recognize that their relationship develops on four planes: the *spiritual*, the *emotional*, the *mental*, and the *physical*. When the first three are in sync, and love has a chance to blossom on its own, the physical part can be the icing on the cake. It is something wonderful, designed by the Creator to help deepen the relationship between two who have pledged themselves to each other totally.

So let's take a close look at perhaps the most beautiful love story of all time, straight from the Word of God—and thus ultimately from the mind and heart of God. I pray that Solomon's Song will be as meaningful to you and your beloved as it has been to Pearl and me. And maybe, just maybe, the wives out there reading this will echo the opinion of a woman attending one of my classes. After we had concluded our study of the Song, this lady exclaimed, "I didn't know I was supposed to expect all of this!" The tragedy is that most of us never do.

4

Courtship

Song 1:1–2:17

From the pages of history and the texts of fairy tales they emerge. We watch their stories unfold on the silver screen and the color television. We read of their passion in Shakespeare and Scripture. Who are they?

They are Antony and Cleopatra, Nicholas and Alexandra, Cinderella and Prince Charming. They are Grace and Rainier, Liz and Dick, Gable and Lombard. They are Romeo and Juliet, Jacob and Rachel, Ruth and Boaz. They are the great lovers, past and present, from the annals of history or the pages of fiction. And to their number must be added the names of still another couple: Solomon and Shulamith.

The account of the king and the girl from the hills of Lebanon rivals that of any romantic novel or ballad. It is all the more compelling because it is not fiction, but poetic truth—a delicate rendition of moments from the lives of two lovers. Solomon's Song is the incomparable record of this romance, which took place long ago in a palace in Jerusalem and in the countryside of Baal-hamon and which was witnessed with approval by a loving and holy God.

We're going to watch the wonder unfold as we peek into the love diary of the king and his bride, beginning with a look at their days of courtship. Maybe we too will recall the almost painful beauty and intensity of the period of courtship, the moment of marriage, the months of newlywed discovery—tender reminiscences which probably have been too long lodged in a remote section of our memory.

If the recollections are pleasant, they can serve to revitalize our relationship as we fondly remember the thrills, chills, and goose-bumps of courtship and early marriage. If the memories are tainted by guilt and regret, then the opportunity is here for each of us to confess the wrong turns of the past, apologize, forgive, and make a brand new beginning in the present. That means making a renewed commitment to the one we married in the first place—starting over, together. It's totally possible, with God (see Isaiah 1:18).

Let's look now at the beginnings of this great love story. I am indebted to S. Craig Glickman whose work, *A Song for Lovers*, contains the translation of Solomon's Song that we will be using, and which is filled with refreshing insights into the text.

Missing Him—Song 1:1-4

1:1 The Song of Songs which is Solomon's.
Bride (in soliloquy)
2 Oh, that he would kiss me with the kisses of his
mouth, for better than wine is your affection.
3 For fragrance your perfumes are pleasing,
and perfume poured forth is your name.
Therefore, the maidens love you.
4 Draw me after you! Let us run together!
The king has brought me to his chambers.

Scene One of our real-life romance opens in Jerusalem, at the king's palace or, as Shulamith puts it, his "chambers" (1:4). There we catch the bride-to-be in a moment of high anxiety. The young maiden has so impressed Solomon on his business trips to Lebanon, that he has arranged for the royal camel caravan to journey north and escort her to the capital for a visit. The country girl has come to the big city for the very first time. She is seeing the sights, the splendor, the opulence of the kingdom and the court. And going uptown has literally overwhelmed her.

She softly speaks to herself these words of longing in

verse 2: "Oh, that he would kiss me with the kisses of his mouth, for better than wine is your affection." Everything is so new, so strange, so different at the court, that all Shulamith can think of is her beloved Solomon, who at the moment is more busy with affairs of state than with affairs of the heart. She yearns for his tender embrace, thirsts for his kisses, which to her are more tantalizing than the sweetest wine. She wants him to be close to her physically. Although they are not yet married and lovemaking is out of the question, she wants to be aroused. Shulamith wants all of that, yes, but what she most deeply desires is Solomon's undivided attention.

The palace is not Lebanon. There the lovers could wander aimlessly among the trees of the forest. They could walk and talk and gaze into each other's eyes. They could pick flowers and throw stones into streams. They could watch billowy clouds waft across the sky. They could be together nearly as much of the time as they wished.

In Jerusalem, things are different. Undersecretaries, ambassadors, military advisers, soldiers, servants, ladies-in-waiting, press agents, and reporters flitter about in a frenzy of activity. The demands of the kingdom pull and tug and tear at Solomon, preventing him from spending as much time with his beloved as both would like. For Shulamith, it is a foretaste of what life will be like married to the chief executive. She longs for the time and attention of her absent lover. She is lonely.

"For fragrance your perfumes are pleasing," Shulamith continues to muse in verse 4. She recalls his scent, and evidently Solomon took care of himself. He'd shower and shampoo before coming to see her, and he'd splash on pleasant-smelling cologne. His desire was to be well-groomed, attractively packaged for his sweet lady.

But her lover's outward appearance matters far less to Shulamith than his inner self, for as she reflects further, she remarks of Solomon, "Perfume poured forth is your name. Therefore the maidens love you" (1:3). In other words, his character is fragrant to her; his personality attracts her. What he is inside is more important than what he looks like or smells like on the outside. She trusts and respects him.

These qualities of character have also spurred the admiration of the maidens of the court, and no doubt Shulamith feels threatened by their affection for her man. What woman wouldn't feel a bit insecure if her very appealing fiance were surrounded by gorgeous secretaries? It is the richness of his character which the women find so compelling and which Shulamith herself discovers to be irresistible.

That brings to mind what, to me, was the most touching part of our daughter Donna's wedding to our son-in-law Mark: the moment when they recited their vows to each other. They had written the words themselves, and it was heartwarming to listen to Donna express to Mark that she loved him because of the quality of his character which had been reflected in their courtship. Essentially, she told him at the altar, "Mark, it's what you are that I love more than what you do." And that's precisely how Shulamith feels about Solomon.

As she realizes the intensity of her emotions, Shulamith exclaims, "Draw me after you! Let us run together!" (1:4). In delight and longing she wishes Solomon would clasp her hand and lead her from the palace halls. With her lover beside her, she longs to flee that strange place. How wonderful it would be if together they could run through the countryside as they had in Lebanon! With the child-like glee which comes with being in love, she desires nothing more than to playfully frolic in the park with her beloved, sharing him with no one else.

Doesn't that remind you of your own days of dating and engagement? You just wanted to be alone with your girl-friend, your boyfriend! You craved time together, hours spent away from parents, teachers, roommates, friends, and little brothers and sisters who had obviously never heard that "two's company, three's a crowd." You wanted to sit together on the porch swing and take drives in the moonlight, share sundaes at the malt shop, sodas at the drive-in, and benches at the park. You only had eyes for each other—and nobody had ever held as much fascination for you as that young man or woman you wanted to marry! The first four verses of the Song show us that Shulamith's feelings are exactly the same.

MEASURING UP—SONG 1:4-11

> *Daughters of Jerusalem to King*
>> We will rejoice and be glad in you.
>> We will extol your love (better) than wine.
> *Bride (in soliloquy)*
>> Rightly do they love you.
> *to Daughters of Jerusalem*
> 5 Dark I am but lovely, O daughters of Jerusalem,
>> like the tents of Kedar,
>> like the curtains of Solomon.
> 6 Do not stare at me for I am dark;
>> the sun has scorched me.
>> My mother's sons were angry with me.
>> They appointed me caretaker of the vineyards,
>>> but of my own vineyard—which belongs to me—I have not taken care.
> *(in soliloquy)*
> 7 Tell me, O you whom my soul loves,
>> where you pasture your flock,
>> where you rest them at noon,
>>> lest I become as a veiled woman by the flocks of your companions.
> *Daughters of Jerusalem to Bride*
> 8 If you do not know, O most beautiful among women, go forth on the trail of the flock
>> and pasture your young goats by the tents of the shepherds.
> *King to Bride*
> 9 To a mare among the chariots of Pharaoh
>> I liken you my darling.
> 10 Lovely are your cheeks with ornaments
>> and your neck with strings of beads.
> *Daughters of Jerusalem to Bride*
> 11 Chains of gold will we make for you
>> with points of silver.

Shulamith's romantic reflections abruptly end as the women of the court interrupt her with words directed to the king: "We will rejoice and be glad in you. We will extol your love better than wine." Oh yes, these women are attracted to Solomon. They praise his love; they take delight in his presence; they rejoice in his company. They are enamored of him because of the kind of person that he is, not just because of his title, power, wealth, or prestige. "Rightly do they love you," sighs Shulamith in the face of the competition (1:4). What a wail of insecurity escapes her lips!

She then turns to the women of the court, confronting the gaggle of jealous females who probably can't imagine why the king has overlooked them and chosen a simple, rustic maiden for his bride. "Dark I am but lovely, O daughters of Jerusalem, like the tents of Kedar, like the curtains of Solomon," she tells them in verse 5. "Do not stare at me for I am dark; the sun has scorched me," she warns them (1:6). Shulamith feels ill at ease among these fair-skinned creatures who gaze at her with disdain. Her suntanned complexion contrasts sharply with their alabaster skin. Her own brownness brings to Shulamith's mind the dark dwellings of the desert nomads. She feels as conspicuous among the court pale-faces as if she were a black tent pitched against a sand-colored landscape.

Shulamith manages to retain some measure of self-confidence, for she tells the women that she is lovely. But as she compares herself to the rich fabric of the draperies in the king's palace, we sense that she is desperately trying to convince herself—or them—that she belongs there. She feels unworthy and out-of-place, well aware of the contempt with which the women view her.

Of course Shulamith doesn't look like the sleek, smooth-skinned beauties of the palace. Her upbringing had been completely different from theirs. She hadn't had time to loll around in perfumed baths. No servants had massaged her skin with fragrant oils, given her mud-pack facials, or manicured her nails. On the contrary, she had been expected to work . . . and work hard!

"My mother's sons were angry with me," she defensively reveals. "They appointed me caretaker of the vineyards, but of my own vineyard—which belongs to me—I have not taken care" (1:6). While growing up, Shulamith had to labor in the fields, forced by her brothers (or stepbrothers) to work there. She did not have the kind of time to spend on her own "vineyard"—her own appearance—that the palace pretties had enjoyed. She hadn't been able to primp and preen, or to experiment with cosmetics and coiffures. With her hair pulled back and twisted into a simple knot so that it would stay out of her eyes, she had sweated in the sun while doing the rough work of a farmhand. She didn't need exercise classes or weights to tone her muscles; her tautness came from tough labor.

And Keeping Up Appearances

Shulamith finishes her defensive speech and turns from her rivals. Then, either speaking to herself or perhaps addressing the king who has entered the room, she asks, "Tell me, O you whom my soul loves, where you pasture your flock, where you rest them at noon, lest I become as a veiled woman by the flocks of your companions" (1:7). In short, she expresses a desire to know where she can find Solomon during working hours without wasting any time. Young lovers today exchange telephone numbers, swap school and work schedules, and plan points of rendezvous so precious minutes together won't be lost. Even old married folks like to know where they can reach each other during the day!

Please don't think that Shulamith asks Solomon for his daily schedule simply so that she can keep tabs on him. Her reasons extend far beyond that, and reflect the high standards of her character. Shulamith wants to know where she can easily find her beloved because she doesn't want to be mistaken for a "veiled woman" (in their culture, a prostitute) chasing after the king. She is concerned about her reputation, and she is also thinking of Solomon's standing with his people. A monarch who plans to marry a streetwalker would indeed appear foolish in the eyes of his subjects! Shulamith prefers to prevent any such ill-founded rumors from hitting the gossip columns.

There is, perhaps, one more reason why the beautiful bride-to-be desires to know Solomon's whereabouts. Deep down inside, maybe even unbeknownst to herself, she longs to be convinced that she is so important to him that she can interrupt his routine. She wants to know that Solomon will put business on hold for a time if she needs something. She yearns to believe that she is top priority in his life. Keeping her well informed of his schedule is one way in which Solomon can reassure Shulamith of his affection. She deserves to be treated with courtesy and honor. Besides, it would be embarrassing for the future wife of a king to have to track him down like a bloodhound in order to talk with him!

I think all husbands can learn something from Shulamith's request. Think about it, men . . . does your wife think she can comfortably contact you during the day? Does she feel she can interrupt your work when necessary? Do you phone her from the office to see how things are going at home (without asking what came in the mail or what's for dinner!)? If it isn't convenient to call, or if you're worried about what the boss will think, then work out an acceptable schedule for touching base with each other. I try to call Pearl before every class I teach, because she is my prayer support—besides, there's no such thing as too much checking in! Why not seriously consider making yourself accessible to your wife? It's important; it tells her that she is number one on your list.

ONE IN A MILLION

Shulamith badly needs to know that she is valuable and precious to Solomon. Immediately after she voices her wish to know of his daily routine, the women of the court reply, using these words laced with sarcasm: "If you do not know, O most beautiful among women, go forth on the trail of the flock and pasture your young goats by the tents of the shepherds" (1:8).

Let's remember that Shulamith earlier defended herself by telling the court ladies that she was attractive; hence, they snidely refer to her as the "most beautiful among women," when they respond to her remarks (1:8). And just look at their so-called advice. According to these catty females, if Shulamith wants to know where to find Solomon, she should take her own little herd of goats and follow the trail of the king's flock. She's such a country girl that she ought to feel right at home pasturing her billy goats by the shepherds' tents! With these caustic comments the palace belles remind Shulamith of her rural background. They know she doesn't fit in with the sophisticated court crowd, and they'd like to keep it that way. Shulamith must feel miserable, nearly desperate for acceptance and reassurance—much like Cinderella surrounded by the sisters ugly.

Like so many other women, Shulamith needs a boost of confidence in the areas of self-image and security. She desires to feel that she is priceless and beautiful. She longs to know that Solomon will not reject her but will remain staunchly by her side always. How fortunate for her that the king is listening.

From Solomon's words in verses 9 and 10, it is obvious that he has overheard Shulamith's musings and has listened to the cutting remarks of the women of the court. We'll see if he is a sensitive lover; if so, he will realize that his lady needs to be built up emotionally by honest words of praise and appreciation. She is in an awkward and awful situation. The sirens are screaming . . . it is up to him to come to the rescue.

If ever there is a perceptive lover, it is Solomon! Gazing into the eyes of Shulamith, he speaks to her so that all might hear: "To a mare among the chariots of Pharaoh I liken you my darling" (1:9). Isn't that incredibly romantic? You're probably thinking what many members of my classes do when we get to that verse: what do you mean, "romantic"? How can comparing her to a horse make her feel good?

Before we go any further, let me warn you not to try the same compliment on your wife, men! The only woman I know who would fall for that one is Gloria Tjoelker, the wife of one of our staff members. Gloria's husband, Pete, has worked with horses most of his life. He loves them, and deeply appreciates the uniqueness and value of a prized mare. Solomon does too, and his comment to Shulamith is really a deep and heartfelt accolade.

Solomon himself owned thousands of horses. They gave tangible evidence of his military might and prowess. The chariots of Pharaoh were pulled by Egyptian stallions, animals highly valued by Solomon. To say that Shulamith is as a priceless mare among such well-bred, spirited equines is high praise indeed.

How much Shulamith needs to hear these words! Solomon doesn't care if there is a bevy of beauties bouncing around his palace. She is the only one who matters, the only woman who appeals to him and excites him and enchants him.

Perhaps Solomon is reminiscing about the days of early courtship when he later pens Proverbs 31:29, where he writes of the excellent wife: "Many women do noble things, but you surpass them all" (NIV). Certainly in the days of his youth, Shulamith holds the sole key to his heart. She transcends all others.

PRAISE HER! PRAISE HER!

Solomon continues to build up the self-image and security of his wife-to-be. In verse 10 we read that he tells her, "Lovely are your cheeks with ornaments and your neck with strings of beads." He praises her choice of jewelry, noticing a "little thing" about her appearance which becomes a big thing as he calls attention to it. No doubt her face flushes with satisfaction at this obvious compliment. She has chosen her accessories wisely; they are appropriate adornment for life at the palace. She does, after all, fit in.

Looking on, the women of the court notice the esteem with which the king treats Shulamith. They begin to view her with increased respect. No longer do they fire sarcastic verbal darts in her direction, but instead they offer to create additional necklaces and charms for her. "Chains of gold will we make for you with points of silver," they tell her (1:11). She has become far more than a country bumpkin in their eyes; she is the beloved of the king.

Solomon has focused on an integral principle of love and marriage: it is vital that a man publicly praise the woman he loves. In his classic bestseller, *Letters to Philip*, pastor Charlie Shedd writes his soon-to-be-wed son a letter of advice on how to make a woman feel extra-special. Here is a selection from his list of suggestions guaranteed to make a woman glow. They are priceless, surefire ways to move a marriage toward greater intimacy.

When you enter the room, take her arm and come in smiling. If you look happy, she will, and God knows the world needs encouragement.

Say something nice when you introduce her. I mean about her. This is good practice and it lifts her spirits. If you make her feel good, you feel good also.

When you sit down to dinner, hold her chair! Then pat her on the shoulder and smile. Keep smiling till she looks up. She'll soon catch on and it becomes a ritual. This is a very good thing.

When the conversation lags, ask her a question! Be sure you choose one she can answer. Make it one of her favorite subjects and always wait for her reply. Never forget, smart people make others feel smart.

Never, and I mean never, fuss over little points in her story. Who cares whether the roses were true pink or only a faded red? If she is all wrong, somebody else can set her straight. But not you.

After dinner, if you get separated, look her up once in a while. Be sure she is pleasantly situated. Tell her you missed her and is she all right?

When you are ready to go, hold her coat, take her arm, and open the car door for her! Not many men do and she knows it. This makes her somebody special.

Sometime when you are with her mother alone, tell her how much you appreciate her daughter. No woman

alive could keep this to herself, and nothing does more
for your wife than a compliment coming in sideways!
(Shedd 1978, 54-55)

STEPPING OUT IN HIGH SOCIETY—SONG 1:12-14

> *Bride in soliloquy*
> 1:12 While the king was at his table,
>   my nard gave its fragrance.
>   13 A pouch of myrrh is my beloved to me
>   which lies all night between my breasts.
>   14 My beloved is to me a cluster of henna blossoms
>   in the vineyards of En-Gedi.

As verse 12 opens, Shulamith again begins to speak. The
setting has shifted to a banquet hall. Here, perhaps, the
king will introduce his Lebanese sweetheart to Jerusalem
high society for the first time. Government officials, reli-
gious leaders, social bigwigs, military commanders, and
foreign dignitaries crowd the elegant room. The press is
there too. Nearly everyone in the city is curious about the
little lady who has captivated their ruler.

But the notoriety doesn't seem to disturb Shulamith. She
is not the least bit nervous at the affair. She no longer feels
ill at ease in the midst of the palace opulence. No vestiges of
awkwardness or self-consciousness remain. Why not? The
answer is simple: Solomon's show of love has made her
self-assured and secure. And she only has eyes for her
man!

"While my king was at his table," she says to herself,
"my nard gave its fragrance" (1:12). The soothing fragrance of Shulamith's perfume refreshes her as she watch-
es Solomon sitting at the dining table. The sweetness of her
perfume reminds her of the one she loves, and her attention is drawn to him.

"A pouch of myrrh is my beloved to me which lies all
night between my breasts," she continues in verse 13. Ori-
ental women of Shulamith's day often placed small bags or

sachets of fragrant spices underneath their gown at night. They would awaken the following morning and their body would be perfumed. The scent would linger all day, and we can assume that recollections of her beloved Solomon remain on Shulamith's mind throughout each waking hour as well. He is a constant, fragrant presence in her thoughts.

"My beloved is to me a cluster of henna blossoms in the vineyards of En-Gedi" (1:14), Shulamith sighs to herself at length, smiling at the man she soon will marry. She compares Solomon to a bouquet of henna blossoms, small rose-scented red or white flowers. As always, her thoughts of him are fragrant. The word *vineyard* in verse 14 may also be translated as "oasis." The particular flowers which color Shulamith's reflections are in the oasis of En-Gedi, and that in itself conveys special meaning.

If you should ever be fortunate enough to visit Israel, you will probably have the option of a tour of Masada. Take it, and try to convince your guide to escort your group a bit farther to En-Gedi. As you climb, you will encounter a place of sheer loveliness. It is a green jewel of waterfalls, grasses, and trees rising above a sizzling wasteland. Truly a refreshing retreat, it is a hideaway from the searing sun. As Shulamith dwells on the qualities of her lover, she realizes that he is as refreshing to her as the coolness of En-Gedi is to the weary, dusty traveler who has crawled forth from the broiling Judean wilderness.

TOGETHER, ALONE, AGAIN—SONG 1:15–2:3

> *King to Bride*
> 1:15 Behold, you are beautiful my darling; behold you
> are beautiful;
> Your eyes are doves.
> *Bride to King*
> 16 Behold, you are handsome my beloved; indeed
> you are pleasant.
> And our couch is verdant.
> 17 The beams of our houses are cedars;
> our rafters, cypresses.

2:1   I am a rose of Sharon,
          a lily of the valley.
King to Bride
2   As a lily among thorns,
          thus is my darling among young women.
Bride (to King)
3   As an apple tree among the trees of the forest,
          so is my beloved among the young men.
      In his shade I took great delight and sat down,
          and his fruit was sweet to my taste.

The setting of the Song changes again as Solomon speaks
in verse 15. Now the couple has temporarily escaped the
confines of the palace. Perhaps they are going for a walk in
one of the gardens surrounding the city of Jerusalem. Or
maybe they are strolling among the cedars and cypresses
of Lebanon. It could be that they have journeyed north
together so that Shulamith might gather belongings and
see relatives or friends. Whatever the case, they are at last
together, alone.

Solomon begins to talk first. I imagine that he touches
Shulamith's face gently with his hands, tilting her chin
upward and caressing her cheek with his fingertips. "Behold, you are beautiful my darling; behold you are beautiful," he tells her. "Your eyes are doves" (1:15).

The eyes are mirrors of the soul; they reveal character.
As Jesus says in Matthew 6:22, "The lamp of the body is
the eye; if therefore your eye is clear, your whole body will
be full of light" (NASB). Shulamith's eyes are clear and soft
and dovelike. They give evidence of her purity and inno-
cence, virginity and gentleness. Often will this pair of
lovers make mention of each other's eyes. Much love can be
expressed by a look.

"Behold, you are handsome my beloved; indeed you are
pleasant," responds Shulamith. "And our couch is verdant.
The beams of our houses are cedars; our rafters, cypresses"
(1:16-17). The lovers stop briefly to lie down. Perhaps she
has packed a picnic basket, and this they begin to share,
throwing themselves back against the soft green carpet of

grass. They gaze upward at the towering trees forming the roof of what has become their imaginary house. The forest is quiet and cool and they are utterly alone.

"I am a rose of Sharon, a lily of the valley," says Shulamith to her lover (2:1). This girl who once was self-conscious because of her tanned skin and simple appearance now thinks of herself as the most beautiful flower in the land of Sharon, an area on the northwest coast of Israel. It is not that she is conceited. Rather, Solomon's demonstrations of affection have made her feel absolutely gorgeous. As a responder, she has begun to perceive herself as he does. She knows she is special to him, and indeed she is precious in his eyes.

Shulamith is not, Solomon assures her, merely as lovely as the rose of Sharon. Why, compared to the other young women in the world, she is as "a lily among thorns" (2:2). She surpasses them all. None of the palace pretties come close to her in beauty or character. She is absolutely superb.

Shulamith compliments the king in turn, telling Solomon that among all young men, he is as "an apple tree among the trees of the forest" (2:3). His fruit is sweet to her taste, and she delights in his shade. She draws energy and vitality and refreshment simply from being with him. In other places in the Song, the apple tree will appear as a symbol of their love.

ALL FLAGS UNFURLED—SONG 2:4-7

> *Bride (in soliloquy)*
> 2:4 He has brought me to the banquet hall,
>   and his banner over me is love.
> *(to King)*
>   5 Sustain me with raisin cakes and refresh me
>   with apples
>   . for I am faint with love.
> *(in soliloquy)*
>   6 Oh that his left hand were under my head and
>   his right hand embraced me.

to Daughters of Jerusalem

   7 I adjure you, O daughters of Jerusalem,
      by the gazelles or the hinds of the field
        not to arouse, not to awaken love until it
        pleases.

Once more the scene shifts in the love diary. Again we are exposed to life in the palace big leagues. Yet now the Shulamith we see is far more confident than she was at her first meeting with the ladies of the court. She is secure in the love of her man.

"He has brought me to the banquet hall, and his banner over me is love" (1:4), she proclaims, perhaps to herself or perhaps so that others might hear. Solomon has shown that he bursts with pride because of her. He has paraded her in front of kings and princes and diplomats. She has attended royal feasts, events of social and political importance. And always, the king has delighted in introducing her to all. Never has he been cold and distant to her in public.

The banner mentioned by Shulamith may have been a reference to one of the huge flags carried into battle by the standard-bearer of Solomon's army. Her comments make me think of our own star-spangled banner. We stand, salute, and sing when our country's flag is unfurled. So proud is Solomon of his future wife that he wouldn't be surprised if she were to evoke the same response from the crowds in Jerusalem. His own chest puffs out with heart-thumping pride when she merely enters a room.

For her part, Shulamith is completely enthralled with the king. She turns to him and asks that he sustain her with fruit, for she is "faint with love" (2:5). She is lovesick—hopelessly, helplessly, totally enamored of him! The attraction increases every day. Quite naturally, she begins to feel desire for the physical.

"Oh that his left hand were under my head and his right hand embraced me," she sighs to herself in verse 6. One would question the authenticity of their love if she does not feel the stirrings of sexual longing. But Shulamith is discreet, pure, and wise. She deserves the high compliments

Solomon has paid her. She is well aware that the time for the physical will be later, after they are married.

She turns to the women of the court and instructs them of the truth of this principle, solemnly swearing by the deer of the field that no one should arouse or "awaken love until it pleases" (2:7). As Solomon himself will later write in the pages of Ecclesiastes, "There is a time for everything, and a season for every activity under heaven" (3:1 NIV). The time for a man and a woman to physically enjoy each other is after they have become husband and wife.

The sexual relationship cannot be awakened prematurely if it is to be all that God intends it to be. When given its proper season, it is an experience as delicious as whipped cream. When forced too soon, it leaves behind the bitter aftertaste of sour milk. Many individuals bear the marks of mistakes they made while courting, when a degree of discipline, a measure of restraint, would have made all the difference. Instead they feel defiled. Sex becomes something dirty, instead of the lovely delight the Lord has designed it to be. Oh yes, it is good not to awaken love before it is pleased to be awakened of itself.

WHILE WAITING—SONG 2:8-17

> *(Bride in soliloquy)*
> 2:8 The sound of my beloved,
>   Behold, he is coming,
>   leaping over the mountains, bounding over the
>   hills.
>   9 My beloved is like a gazelle or a young stag.
>   Look, he is standing behind our wall,
>   gazing through the windows,
>   peering through the lattice.
> 10 My beloved responded and said to me,
>   "Arise my darling, my fair one, and come.
> 11 For behold, the winter has passed.
>   The rain is over and gone.

12 The blossoms have appeared in the land.
   The time of singing has come,
      and the cooing of the turtledove is heard in our
      land.
13 The fig tree forms its figs,
      and the vines in blossom give forth fragrance.
   Arise, my darling, my beautiful one, and come
   along.
14 O my dove, in the clefts of the rocks,
      in the hidden places of the steep pathway,
   Let me see your form; let me hear your voice.
   For your voice is sweet, and your form is lovely.
15 Let us catch the foxes—the little foxes who ruin
   vineyards,
      for our vineyards are in blossom."
16 My beloved is mine and I am his—he who
   pastures his flock among the lilies.
17 Until the day breathes and the shadows flee,
   turn, my beloved, and be like a gazelle or a
   young stag on the mountains of separation.

As chapter 2 continues, Shulamith still speaks in soliloquy. She has evidently returned to Lebanon, and describes
a visit paid her there by Solomon. This may well have been
the occasion when he officially asked for her hand in marriage. It is a tender and precious memory in their album of
love.

"The sound of my beloved, Behold, he is coming, leaping
over the mountains, bounding over the hills," she says to
herself in verse 8. She anticipates his arrival, and it is
amusing and exciting to her to picture his hurried journey.
She is speaking figuratively here of her lover who, like
Superman, will leap tall buildings ("mountains") and out-
run steaming locomotives ("bounding over the hills") in
order to reach her side. Remember how you once said to
your own young love, "I would swim the deepest ocean for
you; I would climb the highest mountain; not wind, rain,
snow, or fire can keep me from your doorstep"? Such

thoughts may well be running through Solomon's mind, too.

Certainly he travels quickly. Shulamith likens him to a swift, sure-footed deer of the forest, a gazelle or young stag (2:9). And then she describes the wonderful moment of his arrival.

"Look, he is standing behind our wall, gazing through the windows, peering through the lattice," Shulamith recalls (2:9). Like Romeo straining for a glimpse of Juliet on the balcony, he cannot wait to catch sight of his beloved. He longs to feast his eyes upon her . . . and why not? It is spring, the season for lovers.

Solomon speaks at last. "Arise my darling, my fair one, and come. For behold the winter has passed" (2:10-11), he tells her. As his words in verses 12-13 reveal, it is the time for blossoms and singing. The cooing of the turtledove can be heard in the land. The buds burst forth on the fig tree, soon to be laden with fruit. Spring is in the air and, like most people in love, Solomon has become incredibly sensitive to the beauty around him.

Love does that. Being in love sharpens the senses, intensifies our awareness of nature. Even the most "macho" males succumb to the enchantment of springtime love. I remember visiting with Tommy Maxwell, former Baltimore Colts cornerback, one March afternoon. Tommy and his wife Janice were living in Dallas at the time, while he attended Dallas Seminary. As he turned to leave at the conclusion of our chat, I called after him, "Where are you headed?"

"Janice and I are going down to look at the roses," he replied. And I thought: Is that big, gruff football player going to gaze at some flowers with his sweetheart? Yes! Love makes everything seem new and fresh and inviting.

Shulamith drinks in these next words of Solomon. "O my dove, in the clefts of the rocks, in the hidden places of the steep pathway, Let me see your form; let me hear your voice. For your voice is sweet, and your form is lovely" (2:14). She is his precious, gentle, graceful dove, and he wants merely to look at her, to capture a vision of her loveliness and indelibly imprint it on his mind. He longs to hear her voice, sweet as a sparkling brook.

We can identify with Solomon in this. Why else do we prop a photo of our loved one on our desk? Why do we look forward to the ringing of the phone, hoping that at the other end will be the voice of our beloved? It's because of the thrill of it all! Hearing Shulamith's voice and seeing her lovely form send joy cascading through Solomon. Their love is a priceless treasure.

THE LITTLE FOXES

So important is their relationship, that Solomon clearly recognizes the need to guard it against outside danger. "Let us catch the foxes—the little foxes who ruin vineyards, for our vineyards are in blossom," he urges (2:15). It is their vineyard or garden of love which begins to bloom in these days of courtship. Yet what are the "little foxes"?

The little foxes drive wedges of separation between two lovers. They threaten to wither the budding flower of love before its petals have a chance to unfold. They creep into a relationship—testing it, weakening it. If unchecked, they can destroy it. Included among them are uncontrolled desire, jealousy, mistrust, selfishness, pride, greed, and bitterness. In fact, I'd say that most of the little foxes fit into one of the following categories:

1. *Sloth.* The "I'm tired of serving, and I just don't care any more" attitude can be fatal to a marriage. It indicates that one or both partners have become lazy, indifferent, weary of well-doing, tired of giving.

2. *Sex.* If the physical relationship is forced prematurely, misused, abused, handled without sensitivity, the stage is set for trouble.

3. *Silver.* When the quest for the almighty dollar consistently consumes more energy than is poured into

making a relationship last, difficulty is inevitable. Priorities are fouled up when we are married to materialism instead of to each other.

4. *Selfishness.* When the questions, "What about me? What am I getting out of this? I want to think of myself once in awhile!" are voiced, the speaker has ceased to be a lover. He (or she) has become more concerned with his own needs than with the needs of his partner.

5. *Satan.* He is the ultimate "fox" of all, and no small one. If he is allowed to gnaw away at a couple's spiritual life, then they forget to pray and they neglect to read God's Word together. Disaster may loom not so very far away.

We must beware of the little foxes. Solomon maintains that defending against such invaders must be a mutual endeavor. The lovers must join together to ward off the danger. Let us capture that which threatens, he implores.

Sheldon "Van" Vanauken and his wife Davy well understood such dangers as those represented by the little foxes. In the earliest dawning of their radiant love, they raised what they called the "Shining Barrier" to protect it. The Shining Barrier—a shield guarding their affection—was created to stand against all selfishness and separateness. As Vanauken writes in *A Severe Mercy,* the story of his life with Davy:

> We raised the Shining Barrier against creeping separateness, which was, in the last analysis, self. We also raised it against a world of indecencies and decaying standards, the decline of courtesy, the whispering mockers of love. We would have our own standards. And, above all, we would be *us*-centred, not self-centred (Vanauken 1981, 29).

The decision to be *us*-centered rather than self-centered is one which all lovers should make early on in their relationship. It is a method of trapping the little foxes which might attempt to wreak havoc. The Vanaukens' Shining Barrier held firm in their years together. Only Davy's untimely and tragic death would separate the couple—in this world, at least. Eventually they will be together again in eternity, for both Van and Davy were privileged to know Jesus Christ as Savior.

In a poignantly beautiful poem, the Vanaukens capture the essence of their definition of love and commitment.

> This present glory, love, once-given grace,
> The sum of blessing in a sure embrace,
> Must not in creeping separateness decline
> But be the centre of our whole design.
>
> We know it's love that keeps a love secure,
> And only by love of love can love endure,
> For self's a killer, reckless of the cost,
> And loves of lilactime unloved are lost.
>
> We build our altar, then, to love and keep
> The holy flame alight and never sleep:
> This darling love shall deepen year by year,
> And dearer shall we grow who are so dear.
>
> The magic word is *sharing*: every stream
> Of beauty, every faith and grief and dream;
> Go hand in hand in gay companionship—
> In sober death no sundering of the grip.
>
> And into love all other loveliness
> That we can tease from time we shall impress:
> Slow dawns and lilacs, traceries of the trees,
> The spring and poems, stars and ancient seas.
>
> This splendour is upon us, high and pure
> As heaven: and we swear it shall endure:
> Swear fortitude for pain and faith for tears
> To hold our shining barrier down the years.
>
> (Vanauken 1981, 47-48)

MINE, ALL MINE

As Solomon and Shulamith's own relationship deepens, their commitment to each other increases. "My beloved is mine and I am his," Shulamith reflects in verse 16. As she does so, I picture her sitting at a desk, writing a page in her diary. Solomon is nearby. Perhaps Shulamith pauses and flashes her engagement ring in the light, watching it sparkle and shine. Her words are evidence that the decision to commit herself totally to him has been made. Exactly when it happened, we are not sure, but she has accepted his proposal—for better or worse, for richer or poorer, in sickness or health, till death's curtain descends. The phrase she uses to express their unity will appear three times in the Song. In each instance in which Shulamith muses that she belongs to Solomon and he to her, we see proof of her mounting affection and growing sense of security.

With, perhaps, a smile playing about her lips, she voices the final wish which closes chapter 2. "Until the day breathes and the shadows flee, turn, my beloved, and be like a gazelle or a young stag on the mountains of separation," she requests in verse 17. In her delicate fashion, Shulamith reveals that she desires that Solomon consummate their marriage—throughout the wedding night until the next morning, when the "day breathes and the shadows flee." The "mountains of separation" are a tasteful reference to her breasts. The longing for the physical expression of their love is becoming increasingly more intense to her.

How special it is that Shulamith does not think she must hide her yearnings. She can mention the physical, and not worry about Solomon's taking advantage of the situation. She feels safe and secure and free to verbalize her desires at the close of their courtship scene. He has earned her respect and her trust.

LESSONS

Many lessons emerge from these days of early romance. Let's look at a few.

Lesson one: *true love heightens the self-image.* Solomon assures Shulamith that she is the loveliest flower of all, matchless and incomparable. And she begins to see herself as he does.

Lesson two: *love must blossom of its own accord.* We musn't attempt to awaken it prematurely—it must bloom in its proper season.

Lesson three: *both partners must watch out for the little foxes which can spoil a relationship.*

Lesson four: *it is what a man is more than what a man does that makes him a lover.*

Lesson five: *a genuine lover is a sensitive servant.*

Lesson six: *the woman is designed by God to respond to what she receives.*

FOOD FOR THOUGHT

The Song of Solomon speaks to more than our marriage, although that is its chief purpose. We can learn much spiritually from the Bible's greatest romance.

Perhaps the most important lesson grasped thus far by the king and his bride-to-be is that they must capture the little foxes which may threaten to ravage their relationship. The creatures must be corralled before the damage is irreparable. So too must we as Christians be on the look-out for the little foxes which may creep into our relationship with the Lord. Unchecked sins can eventually devastate us spiritually. Here are a few foxes I suggest we set out to stalk:

1. *Overt sin.* Our relationship with the Lord will be damaged if we willfully persist in doing something we know to be wrong. Likewise it will suffer if we refuse to do what we know to be right. As James 4:17 states, "Anyone, then, who knows the good he ought to do and doesn't do it, sins" (NIV).

2. *Doubt.* We must catch the fox of doubt. It will nibble at our faith as we begin to question God's power and mercy and goodness. The second part of Ro-

mans 14:23 tells us that "everything that does not come from faith is sin" (NIV). Let's not forget that.

3. *Favoritism.* Parents sometimes play favorites with their children. Men and women caught up in climbing the social ladder frequently ignore those "beneath" them. But it is sin if we are partial to some people and disdainful of others. As James 2:9 puts it, "But if you show favoritism, you sin and are convicted by the law as lawbreakers" (NIV).

4. *Finances.* A fourth fox is seen in the area of our financial stewardship. 2 Corinthians 9:7 contains these instructions: "Each man should give what he has decided in his heart to give, not reluctantly or under compulsion, for God loves a cheerful giver" (NIV). Often we sing, "Were the whole realm of nature mine, that were a present far too small," and we end up putting only a dollar bill in the collection plate.

The four foxes mentioned above are just some of many which may nibble and gnaw at the vines of our relationship with the Lord. Although as Christians our ultimate salvation is assured, if we're guilty of allowing any such predators free rein in our spiritual life, then our fruitfulness for God will be greatly reduced. We must deal with the small sins before they become big sins and thus destroy our effectiveness for God. That means confessing them and turning from them with the help of Jesus Christ. The little foxes are an ever-present threat, both to a marriage and to a life lived for Him.

Questions for Personal or Group Study

1. Why does Shulamith feel inferior to the women of the court when she first arrives there? (See Song 1:1-8.) How does Solomon sensitively respond to her feelings of insecurity in verses 9-10 of chapter 1?

2. As chapter 2 opens, how has Shulamith's opinion of herself changed? What has brought about this transformation?

3. What advice does Shulamith give to the ladies of the palace in Song 2:7? Do you agree? Why or why not?

4. What is meant by Solomon's statement, "Let us catch the foxes—the little foxes who ruin vineyards, for our vineyards are in blossom" (2:15)? Can you name any "foxes" which may have made inroads into your married life? Your spiritual life?

5. From Shulamith's final statement in chapter 2, is she experiencing the demands for the physical? Do you think she is handling her desires properly? Explain.

5

Commitment

Song 3:1–5:1

Before class one evening, a lady shared with me the news that her ten-year-old daughter had been reading through the Bible on her own. I was clearly impressed, and she continued her story, smiling as she spoke. It seems that when the girl had arrived at chapter 4 of the Song of Solomon, she carried her open Bible to her mother and, with wide eyes, exclaimed, "Mom, should I really be reading this?"

I had to laugh at that! Yet it also made me stop and think. Most parents agree that the days of childhood fly by with amazing—and disconcerting—speed. Ten-year-olds become teenagers before Mom and Dad are ready. The teen years pass in a flurry of activity: drivers' licenses are earned, proms attended, graduation survived, and college begun. As their youngsters bound breathlessly into adulthood, parents straggle behind wondering where the time went. And somewhere in this confused and confusing process of growing up, young people experience the flush of first love.

Teenagers are well able to identify with the emotions and longings expressed by two lovers on their wedding night. How vital it is that we instruct our children about the importance of sexual restraint and discipline, so that as adults they, like Shulamith, may experience the innocent joy of total giving, within the bond of marriage. As we'll see in chapter 4 of the Song of Solomon, the wedding night is all that it should be for our hero and heroine . . . and more.

THE EMPTINESS OF PARTIAL COMMITMENT

Physical giving is only part of a marriage. As we saw in the account of Ruth and Boaz, with a relationship must come responsibility. With the confession of love and desire must come a willful commitment. Modern society distorts the picture, presenting casual sex as acceptable. Those who are slightly more conservative claim, "Making love is okay, as long as you really love each other." The Bible offers another view. Sexual intimacy is designed for husbands and wives only. That is why we shall continue to see Solomon and Shulamith exercise self-control until they are wed.

But even saying "I do" at the altar isn't enough. There must be a total commitment of the heart, of the mind, and of the will. Lovemaking under any other conditions is not that at all. It is sex which is selfish and hurtful and ugly.

Perhaps nowhere in Scripture does that become more evident than in the story of Jacob and Leah. Let's briefly refresh our memories about the account in Genesis 28–30. You recall that Jacob, forced to flee the wrath of his brother Esau, sought refuge in the land of his uncle Laban. There he caught sight of Rachel, Laban's younger daughter, and she captured his heart. Jacob agreed to work seven years for his uncle if, at the end of that time, he would be allowed to marry Rachel. As we have discussed previously, the seven years seemed but as a few days for Jacob, because of his great love for the maiden. At last the time for the wedding arrived.

In celebration, Laban threw a huge dinner party, and at the end of the festivities Jacob was given his veiled bride. They adjourned to enjoy the privacy of the wedding night. But as the first rays of sunlight filtered into the newlyweds' tent the next morning, Jacob awoke to receive the shock of his life. Lying next to him was not his beloved Rachel, but her older sister Leah! Laban had deceived him, purposely presenting him with the wrong woman the evening before. The deception had been discovered too late. The damage was done. Leah was his wife. Rachel had probably spent what should have been the happiest night of her life in forced isolation, crying, her eyes awash with disappointment and despair.

Soon Rachel too would be given to Jacob, and until her death she would be the one he cherished. He may have been tricked into marrying Leah, but Rachel was the woman to whom he had committed his heart, mind, and soul. Yet that did not stop him from having sexual relations with his first wife.

Four sons were born to Leah in rather rapid succession; the names she gave them offer eloquent testimony to the misery she knew. Life with a man who could not love her with his whole heart was agonizing. Leah named the first baby she bore Reuben, meaning "the Lord has seen me in my affliction." Her second son was called Simeon or "unloved." The third boy was given the name Levi, or "attached." "Now at last my husband will become attached to me, because I have borne him three sons," Leah said (Genesis 29:34 NIV). The fourth child she called Judah, meaning "God be praised."

Nearly unbearable emotional pain must have blanketed Leah during her first years of marriage. She knew Jacob physically, but there was no real intimacy, no sincere sharing, no genuine satisfaction. He reserved the best of himself for the one he loved most. Rachel possessed his heart; Leah received only remnants of his affection and vestiges of his favor. And as the names of her children suggest, she was desolate in her grief.

A JOYFUL START

The first evening of Solomon and Shulamith's life as husband and wife is vastly different. Unlike Jacob and Leah, they are two people deeply in love, and the start of their lovemaking is sweet. It is the culmination of a relationship which has been developing on emotional, intellectual, and spiritual levels, and to which both bride and groom completely commit themselves.

But before we see the beauty of the wedding night, we

will glimpse two other scenes in the love diary of our couple. The first takes place in Lebanon, as Shulamith awaits the day of her marriage. In the second scene, we shall observe the pageantry of the wedding procession, as that day finally arrives.

YOU'RE TOO GOOD TO BE TRUE—SONG 3:1-5

Bride (in soliloquy)

3:1 Upon my bed in the night I sought him whom
     my soul loves.
    I sought him but did not find him.

2 I will arise now and go about in the city,
     in the streets and in the squares.
    I will seek him whom my soul loves.
    I sought him but did not find him.

3 The watchmen who go about in the city found
    me.
    (I said), "Have you seen him
     whom my soul loves?"

4 Scarcely had I passed from them when I found
     him whom my soul loves.
    I held on to him and would not let him go
     until I brought him to the house of my mother,
     to the room of the one who conceived me.

to the Daughters of Jerusalem

5 I adjure you, O daughters of Jerusalem,
     by the gazelles or the hinds of the field
    not to arouse, not to awaken love until it
     pleases.

As chapter 3 opens, we find Shulamith at home in Lebanon. After weighing the pros and cons of royal life, she has accepted the marriage proposal of Solomon, and he has returned to Jerusalem. There he will attend to business and make arrangements for the upcoming wedding. Meanwhile, she waits.

Being apart from the one you care about is tough any

time, but it is especially so during the period of engage-ment. The questions "Does he love me? Will she say yes?" have already been answered, and all that remains is an excruciating period of waiting for the wedding day.

As we've seen from her last comments in chapter 2, Shulamith's desire for the physical consummation of her relationship with Solomon is building to the boiling point. It's difficult enough to be patient, but now that her beloved has gone back home, her heart aches with anxious longing. She is unbearably lonely, nurtured by thoughts of him, yet missing him terribly. She would like simply to see him again, to touch her lips to his, to hold her hand. It seems as if, in telling him goodbye, she has also bid farewell to a part of herself.

The contents of the following letter probably express the mind and heart of Shulamith as she waits for her lover's return. The note was written by a young woman whose sweetheart had left to return to his home in a distant city. The letter is addressed to him.

Dear Terry,

You've been gone about 3½ hours and I guess you know what's on my mind and heart *now.* I can only trust the Lord to convey to you the way I feel, because I certainly can't. I can only use words, and there aren't any in the English language that quite express how awed I am at the love He has shown me. Why did He choose to bless *me* at this time with you and your love? Why am I so fortunate when there are so many deserving? I am really feeling this tonight. He has given you freely to me because He loves me. You know, that's amazing. I can barely grasp such grace and love. Terry, after you left, I was sort of in a daze for a while and sat outside by myself. Only He kept my emotions under control *while* you were *still* here, because I couldn't have. I sensed His restraining Spirit then, but *soon* as you left He removed the restraint and let me pour out my heart and emotions to Him. My tears weren't because I was desperate or lost, but because I really felt like a part of me was missing (Thomas 1979, 38-39).

That message was sent from Nancy Jane Groover to Terry Thomas. This young couple was deeply in love, and their subsequent wedding was a joyous affair. Nancy, a beautiful girl even in blue jeans and sweatshirt, glowed radiantly in her gown of white. The ceremony was all that it should be and could be, and the wedding night left Terry with memories to last a lifetime. They had to last, for that one wonderful, magical night was to be their only one as man and wife. The next day Nancy was killed and Terry severely injured as an oncoming vehicle collided with their compact car on a rainslick freeway.

Terry Thomas has written about the experience of courting, marrying, and losing Nancy in a marvelous book, *At Least We Were Married*, from which the letter reprinted earlier is taken. I recommend the book, not only because of the poignancy of the story, but also because of the tremendous sense of victory it conveys. Terry and Nancy were both devoted Christians and, though death's barrier severed their earthly union, they will ultimately be together again in eternity. In the meantime, it is wonderful to learn of how God's grace and comfort proved sufficient for Terry, even in this worst of all possible crises.

To those of us who fondly recall the anxious moments of the months and days before our own wedding, the Thomases' story is a nightmare come true. But as the title of Terry's book reveals, at least they were married. I wonder how many of us feared that something horrible would happen to our fiance(e) before it was time for the trip to the altar. And how many of us were quietly afraid that there would be a change of heart, that our loved one would break off the relationship, or even jilt us at the church?

My wife, Pearl, had a nagging fear that we would not make it to the ceremony. Do you know what she was afraid would intervene to prevent our marriage? The rapture! She secretly hoped that the Lord would hold off a bit before calling His children home (see 1 Thessalonians 4:16-

17), just long enough so that we could say, "I do." Well, He did—and we did!

Yet the anxiety is there for almost every bride-to-be. If you put yourself in Shulamith's sandals for a moment, you'll understand what she is going through as chapter 3 begins. Here she is, a little girl from Lebanon who has been overwhelmed by the pomp, circumstance, and majesty of the kingdom and the king. Now that she is alone in her home town, it all seems too good to be true. Deep inside she is scared that something will prevent the miracle of marriage to Solomon from taking place. Surely the worst will happen! She has succumbed to a classic case of pre-wedding jitters.

Tossing and Turning

When anxiety levels are high, sleep is often disturbed. So it is with Shulamith, whose slumber is made even more fitful by a nightmare. It is the kind of bad dream from which the dreamer awakes convinced of its reality. Relief gradually washes over the victim as it dawns on him or her that, after all, it was only a dream.

We know that Shulamith is dreaming because she says in verse 1, "Upon my bed at night I sought him whom my soul loves. I sought him but did not find him." She is lying down and, in the midst of her sleep, begins the voyage into the realm of the subconscious. She envisions herself searching the covers desperately for her lover. Of course he isn't there.

So she dreams that she arises, walks about the streets and squares of the city, seeking the one she loves. "I sought him but did not find him," she tells us (3:2). Hazy figures—the watchmen of the city—confront her as the dream continues. "Have you seen him whom my soul loves?" she frantically asks (3:3). They answer only with silence.

She walks away from them . . . and in the surreal world of her imagination, at last she finds her lover! "Scarcely had I passed from them [the watchmen] when I found him whom my soul loves," Shulamith recalls. "I held on to him," she explains, "and would not let him go until I brought him to the house of my mother, to the room of the one who conceived me" (3:4). In her shadowy dreamworld, she clings tightly to her once-lost lover, refusing to let him go. Thus does her subconscious mind offer vivid testimony of her subtle fear that the wedding will never occur.

The women of the court appear next in her dream, and Shulamith turns to them. She cautions them, as she had in Jerusalem, not to awaken love until its proper time. And on that note in verse 5, the vision ends.

I imagine Shulamith then awakens, breathless. Her pounding heart slows as she sighs in relief and release from the tension. "Thank You, Lord, that it was only a dream," she possibly whispers. Soon her nights will be spent in the arms of her lover. Soon Solomon, as was the custom of their culture, will lead the wedding procession to her town, and take her with him to their new home.

HERE COMES THE GROOM—SONG 3:6-11

Poet
3:6   What is this coming from the wilderness
            like columns of smoke,
            from the burning of myrrh and frankincense
            made from all the scented powders of the
                merchant?
7   Behold! It is the couch of Solomon.
        Sixty mighty men around it from the mighty
            men of Israel.
8   All of them wielders of the sword, trained for
            battle;
        Each, his sword at his side
            (for protection) from the terrors of the night.
9   A palanquin King Solomon made for himself
            from the timber of Lebanon.

10 He made its posts of silver, its back of gold,
     its seat of purple cloth, its interior inlaid
     with expressions of love from the daughters
     of Jerusalem.
11 Go forth, O daughters of Zion, and look upon
     King Solomon with the crown with which his
     mother has crowned him on the day of his
     wedding and on the day of the gladness of his
     heart.

Often young lovers keep track of how many weeks, days, and even minutes are left until time for the wedding. As the second scene of this portion of our drama commences, the tense days of waiting are finally over for Shulamith. The countdown is complete; it is time for Solomon to arrive and claim his bride.

From the distance, in the wilderness beyond the city limits of Shulamith's home town, columns of smoke mysteriously arise. Yet no fire blazes in the forest, nor does any invading army march toward the town gate. The billows of smoke have been caused by the burning of incense— "myrrh and frankincense made from all the scented powders of the merchant" (3:6)—and they signal an "invasion" of another kind. King Solomon is coming to fetch his bride. The small town girl has made it big, and all her relatives, friends, and neighbors are witnesses!

"Behold!" the narrator of the Song shouts. "It is the couch of Solomon" (3:7). And what an entourage follows the king along the mountain trail into the city. Sixty well-armed, battle-hardened men march alongside the canopied couch on which Solomon is carried. They are the sixty mightiest warriors in the kingdom of Israel. "All of them," reveals verse 8, are "wielders of the sword, trained for battle." Each soldier carries his sword at his side for protection from "the terrors of the night."

This attachment of "secret service" agents has accompanied Solomon during the two-day journey from Jerusalem, guarding the royal procession against bandits and rebels. They will do the same on the return trip, when Solomon's bride accompanies him. The king is well able to provide for the protection of his future wife. Any modern day groom should be able to follow his example: marrying only when he is capable of materially, emotionally, and spiritually caring for the woman he loves.

As verse 9 reveals, Solomon is carried on a palanquin, or covered litter, which he has specially ordered. It is made "from the timber of Lebanon" (3:9). Evidently, he had arranged for the lumber to be transported south from Lebanon to Israel, and there ordered his craftsmen to build the frame. He knows that Shulamith will recognize the wood, and that the use of fine materials from her native land will be surprising and immensely pleasing to her. How perceptive of the king! It was a relatively little thing (for him) to have had the palanquin constructed of Lebanese timber . . . but oh what a big thing it becomes in the eyes of a lover—a romantic and thoughtful gesture.

The royal couch is a Rolls Royce among covered litters, too. According to verse 12, its posts are made of silver, its back encrusted with gold, its seat upholstered in rich purple fabric—the colors connoting royalty and splendor. The interior of the coach is ornate: "inlaid with expressions of love from the daughters of Jerusalem" (3:11). The women of the court, who have previously mocked and scorned the country girl, now offer their best wishes to the happy couple, demonstrating their affection by decorating the royal carriage.

Solomon spares no expense or detail in providing a luxurious and beautiful transport for his bride. Surely his attention to detail does not stop with the ornate palanquin and impressive procession. The home he has prepared for Shulamith in Jerusalem is probably just as fantastic, with the same degree of beauty and luxury. Nothing is too good for the one he loves.

An amazing thing for us as Christians to realize is that we can expect even greater wonders than these witnessed by Shulamith, when we meet our bridegroom, Jesus Christ, in eternity. How comforting and exciting are Christ's words in John 14:2: "In my Father's house are many mansions; if it were not so, I would have told you. I go to prepare a place for you" (KJV). The everlasting home the Lord has readied for His children makes Solomon's elaborate preparations seem dim and lackluster by comparison.

But in the Song of Solomon, the joy and glory are earthbound. "Go forth, O daughters of Zion, and look upon King Solomon," implores the voice or narrator speaking in this section of the Song (3:11). The king wears a "crown with which his mother has crowned him on the day of his wedding and on the day of the gladness of his heart" (3:11). It is the happiest time of Solomon's life, and his mother Bathsheba has given him a special headpiece marking the blessed occasion.

Joy abounds not only because the king is about to wed the girl of his dreams, but also, and especially, because the entire event lies within the will of God. The Lord approves of the match and of the marriage; Shulamith is the one He intends for Solomon. Were it not so, there would be reservations and misgivings. The happiness would be dulled by uncertainty. The result would eventually, inevitably, be one of tears and regret. It is not so in the case of the king and his bride.

THE WEDDING NIGHT BEGINS—SONG 4:1-8

> *King to Bride*
> 4:1   Behold, you are beautiful, my darling; behold,
>   you are beautiful.
>   Your eyes are doves from behind your veil.
>   Your hair is like a flock of goats which descend
>   from Mount Gilead.
>   2   Your teeth are like a flock of newly shorn sheep
>   which have come up from the washing,
>   all of which are paired,
>   and not one of them is alone.
>   3   Like a scarlet thread are your lips,
>   and your mouth is lovely.
>   Your temples are like a slice of pomegranate
>   behind your veil.

4   Like the tower of David is your neck, built for
    warfare—
      a thousand shields hang upon it,
      all the shields of the mighty men.
5   Your two breasts are like two fawns, twins of a
    gazelle,
      which feed among the lilies.
6   Until the day breathes and the shadows flee,
      I will go my way to the mountain of myrrh
      and hill of frankincense.
7   You are altogether fair, my love, and there is
      no blemish in you.

We don't know anything about the actual wedding of
Solomon and Shulamith, but we do know that they travel
safely back to Jerusalem. There the marriage is solem-
nized. The next scene which we encounter from their diary
of love is the wedding night itself. The ceremony is over,
the evening's feasting concluded, and the king and his new
wife have retired to a chamber in the palace for a night
they'll never forget.

The first seven verses of chapter 4 record words of praise
spoken by Solomon to his beloved bride when they are
finally alone. His comments show him to be a sensitive
lover, fully aware of the delicate blend of tension and passion, nervousness and desire, characteristic of a couple's
first time of lovemaking together. Most brides feel at least a
little insecure on their wedding night . . . and Shulamith
has ample reason to be nervous: after all, she has married
the king, who could have had his pick of women!

"Behold, you are beautiful, my darling; behold, you are
beautiful," he begins in verse 1. Then he echoes the compliment he had paid her during their courtship by saying,
"Your eyes are doves from behind your veil" (4:1; see 2:15).
His image of her has not changed; she is still the innocent,
pure maiden he had walked and talked with in the forest.
Her bright, dove-like eyes show that she is peaceful, soft,
gentle, and alert.

As Solomon speaks those first words of praise, it is obvious that he looks directly into Shulamith's eyes, and that she returns his gaze. His remarks come from the heart; they are honest compliments given without ulterior motive. She, too, can face him openly. Her motives in marrying him have been innocent. She has pledged herself to him because she loves him, not because she craves the prestige, wealth, and position that only a queen may enjoy.

On this night of nights, there is no need for the visual evasion—glances to the side, downcast eyes—which comes when bitterness, anger, and dishonesty have crept into a relationship. When we tell the truth, we are able to look directly into the eyes of the one we address. When we are less than candid, we cannot squarely face another; we hedge and hesitate; we look away. Not so with Solomon, who gazes intently at his lovely bride.

"Your hair is like a flock of goats which descend from Mount Gilead," he tells her in verse 1. That hardly sounds like a compliment, but remember that Shulamith has been raised in a rural environment. The picture of goats moving downhill after a day's grazing is a vivid image in her mind. From a distance at sunset, such a flock would appear to be an undulating mass of shimmering blackness. Her hair is like this to him—thick and full, wavy and shiny, captivating his attention.

Solomon pays his bride another seemingly unlikely compliment in verse 2. "Your teeth are like a flock of newly shorn sheep which have come up from the washing, all of which are paired, and not one of them is alone," he says. Again he appeals to her rustic nature. Her teeth are as smooth and white as sheep which have been freshly clipped and bathed. They are perfectly matched, too. None are oversized, and not one is missing.

Perhaps by these comments the king also suggests something about Shulamith's smile. Glickman paraphrases verse 2 this way: "Your full and lovely smile is as cheerful and sparkling as pairs of young lambs scurrying up from a washing" (Glickman 1976, 144). Her smile is sweet and playful; simply watching it lightens Solomon's heart and refreshes him.

"Like a scarlet thread are your lips, and your mouth is

lovely," he goes on to say (4:3). Shulamith's lips are well-formed and distinct, outlined delicately as if with a thread. My wife tells me that many women use a red pencil to sketch the outline of their mouth. Then they color in the space with lipstick. Maybe Shulamith wore some touches of make-up to bed. At least one lady I know does this for her husband. His work schedule is such that she often only sees him in the late evening, so she applies cosmetics before turning in. This wife has spent more cash on certain night-gowns than she has on dresses. She wants to look her best for her man.

So does Shulamith. And to Solomon she is incredibly beautiful. Behind her veil, her temples—or cheeks—shine like "a slice of a pomegranate," as he further remarks (4:3). They are rosy, flushed with health, beauty . . . and excitement. She is a blushing bride, if ever there was one!

"Like the tower of David is your neck, built for warfare," Solomon next tells his beloved, "a thousand shields hang upon it, all the shields of the mighty men" (4:4). Until considered more closely, these compliments seem dubious at best. But in likening Shulamith's neck to the tower of David, Solomon probably refers to her strength of character. She is stately and dignified. She holds her head high. When he says her neck is "built for warfare," he likely means that she is strong, capable of enduring testing and hardship. She embodies fortitude. Perhaps he is also suggesting that in her purity, she has resisted the advances of other men, much as the fortress of David stood firm against the onslaught of attacking armies (see 8:8-10). Thus he reassures her that he admires more about her than her beauty.

The "thousand shields" of "mighty men" which hang upon her neck could be a reference to her necklace—perhaps a rope of gold decorated with glittering silver charms, made for her by the women of the court who once mocked her (see 1:11). Maybe he is suggesting that she is noble and precious, worthy of being defended by the mightiest warriors of the land. Either way, she is a lady of remarkable character. What woman wouldn't feel safe and secure, having been treated to such honest words of praise?

Solomon becomes more intimate and erotic in his speech as their passion rises. "Your two breasts are like two fawns, twins of a gazelle, which feed among the lilies," he tells Shulamith in verse 5. Her soft breasts are perfectly matched. He is fond of stroking and caressing them. The sensation of touching them is playfully pleasurable to him—much the same as he might feel when stroking gentle, bright-eyed fawns.

But her breasts also arouse him. "Until the day breathes and the shadows flee, I will go my way to the mountain of myrrh and hill of frankincense," he tells her as their excitement climbs. Remember that in chapter 2, verse 17, Shulamith had shyly voiced her desire for their marriage to be consummated throughout their wedding night. When that splendid time finally arrives, Solomon echoes her words, pledging to fulfill her request. His statement reveals two truths.

First, *he has waited*. This is their first sexual encounter, and he has exercised restraint until now, after the vows have been exchanged.

Second, *he is tremendously sensitive*. Solomon takes the statement of longing and desire which Shulamith made during their courtship, and he brings it into the bedroom on their wedding night. He knows she will recall uttering similar words. He is preparing to do as she asked—and he praises her all the more by his choice of words. Instead of the "mountains of separation" to which she referred, he describes her breasts as "the mountain of myrrh and hill of frankincense." Myrrh and frankincense were items of luxury, imported to Israel at great expense. Shulamith's breasts are therefore of great value to her groom, sweetly intoxicating to him, fragrant as the finest, most expensive spices and perfumes.

He concludes his praise by telling her that, as far as he is concerned, she is absolutely perfect! "You are altogether fair, my love, and there is no blemish in you," says the king (4:7). What a way to make her feel treasured and special, to build her ego! To him, in every way she is flawless, a work of artistic perfection.

How fantastic it would be if each of us were as apprecia-tive of the one we love! Usually we think of our spouse as less than perfect—stuck somewhere between "pretty good" and "needs improvement" on a ratings scale. It is alarm-ingly easy to subtly or overtly convey such dissatisfaction to our mate, too. In writing of her first night as Mrs. Rich-ard Roberts, Patti Roberts tells of an experience which strikes gut-level at insensitive lovers. The following is from *Ashes to Gold.*

> Like most new brides, I had been looking forward eagerly to this night. For the first time in my life, I was going to make love to a man and it was going to be a wonderful thing to do . . . . Richard was going to love me, and maybe that would take this uneasiness out of my heart. Maybe by physically pouring out his love he could take the confusion and fear away from both of us. Maybe we could love it away.
>
> My fantasies were interrupted abruptly when Rich-ard looked up from the bed and said, "You know, you look fatter with your clothes off."
>
> I was devastated. I was self-conscious about my weight anyway. Now I wanted to hide—to cover my nakedness, both physical and emotional—from this man. I did not feel like an adored bride, a precious. love object to my husband. I felt fat and unattractive, and I realized with a sinking feeling in the pit of my stomach that while we might make love on this night, we would not be lovers. We might be physically inti-mate, but there would be no real intimacy between us.
>
> Richard seemed blissfully unaware of the effect his words had produced in me and urged me to come on to bed. I should have shared my feelings with him right then and cleared the air, but I was too hurt. So, I kept silent and we dutifully and rather timidly con-summated our marriage (Roberts 1983, 70-71).

The Robertses' marriage ended tragically in divorce ten years later. Patti's account, in *Ashes to Gold,* of the rise and the demise of her relationship with Richard is an honest and fair appraisal of the wreckage. She shoulders her share of the blame. But on that first night of their marriage, the culprit chipping away at the foundation came in the form of a terribly thoughtless remark.

I wonder how many of us are "blissfully unaware" of the effects our comments have upon those we love? Statements like, "I wish you'd do something about your hair. . . . You're putting on a little weight, honey—I can pinch an inch! . . . Why do you always look so frazzled? . . . Coming to bed with you is like sleeping with a cold fish," have no place in the bedroom (if anywhere). Words of praise and admiration, not jolts of criticism, are appropriate for lovers. If there is an area of weakness we feel compelled to tactfully point out to our spouse, there is a right way and a right time. Offering "helpful" little morsels of advice before lovemaking is tantamount to throwing our mate into a cold shower; any excitement is quickly quenched.

Solomon is much too wise to make such a foolish blunder on his wedding night. And more importantly, the words he speaks are not just empty flattery. He means what he says when he compliments his bride. She is one in a million, to him.

THE WEDDING NIGHT, CONTINUED—SONG 4:8–5:1

King to Bride

4:8   With me from Lebanon, O bride, with me from
          Lebanon come.
          Journey from the peak of Amana,
              from the peak of Senir and Hermon,
              from the dens of lions and the mountains of
              leopards.
   9 · You have made my heart beat fast, my sister, my
          bride.
          You have made my heart beat fast
              with one glance of your eyes,
              with one jewel of your necklace.

10 How beautiful are your caresses, my sister, my
    bride.
How much better are your caresses than wine
    and the fragrance of your perfumes
        than any spice.

11 Your lips, (my) bride, drip honey;
Honey and milk are under your tongue,
    and the fragrance of your garments is like
        the fragrance of Lebanon.

12 A garden locked is my sister, (my) bride.
A spring locked, a fountain sealed.

13 Your shoots are a paradise of pomegranates
    with excellent fruit,
    henna blossoms with nard plants,

14 nard and saffron, calamus and cinnamon,
    with all trees of frankincense,
    myrrh and aloes with all the choicest of
        spices,

15 a garden fountain, a well of living water
and streams flowing from Lebanon.

Bride to King

16 Awake, O north wind.
And come, wind of the south.
Blow upon my garden and let its spices flow
    forth.
May my beloved come to his garden and eat
    its excellent fruit.

King to Bride

5:1 I have come into my garden, my sister, my bride.
I have gathered my myrrh with my balsam.
I have eaten my honeycomb with my honey.
I have drunk my wine with my milk.

Poet to Bride and King

Eat, O loved ones;
Drink and be drunk, O lovers.

After Solomon praises his bride, he makes a request, asking that she turn her thoughts toward him. It is a transitional point in their lovemaking, as he says to her, "With

me from Lebanon, O bride, with me from Lebanon come"
(4:8).

Think about it—only forty-eight hours or so before, she
had been sequestered in her small town, anxiously awaiting his arrival. Her nights had been filled with fearful
dreams, her days with monotony. Now, suddenly, she finds
herself in the arms of the king. Of course she still thinks of
the home she left such a short time before.

Naturally, Solomon, wise husband that he is, desires Shulamith's full attention as they embrace. Many a romantic
moment has been dimmed when visions of dirty dishes,
unfolded laundry, committee meetings, business appointments, and children's problems are permitted to dance in
the heads of the lovers, infiltrating the mood. Lovemaking
at its best and most beautiful calls for the total concentra-
tion of two who are seeking to share and to give and to
enjoy.

When the king asks Shulamith to journey with him
away from "the peak of Amana, from the peak of Senir
and Hermon" (4:8), he is imploring her to leave the images
of her homeland behind. The mountains he mentions are
native to Lebanon. He desires that she focus fully on him
and savor each moment of their sweet, rising passion.

But before Shulamith can do this, she must also leave
behind thoughts of "the dens of lions and the mountains of
leopards" (4:8). These are dreadful places, frightening
memories. She must abandon them in order to drink fully
of their cup of love on this special night. Implied in Solomon's request, I believe, is that she leave behind all fear,
and approach their lovemaking without reservation.

By asking her to forget the lions and leopards, he is
begging her to relax, to set aside any sense of alarm. Most
brides are nervous on their wedding night. The passion is
tempered by tension, the flame defused a bit by the fear of
the unknown. Such insecurity is natural. How sensitive of
Solomon to first build up Shulamith's self-image through
praise and then prepare her emotionally and mentally by
calling her attention to him.

And what an effect she has had on him! "You have made

my heart beat fast, my sister, my bride," he tells her. "You have made my heart beat fast with one glance of your eyes, with one jewel of your necklace" (4:9). A mere glimpse of the jewelry resting upon her neck, a slight look from her eyes—these are enough to excite the bridegroom. He calls Shulamith "my sister," an affectionate term used by men of their culture to describe their wives or female relatives. She is definitely not his flesh-and-blood sister, however, and his thoughts and intentions this night, while honorable, are far from brotherly!

Neither is she placid or restrained in her behavior. "How beautiful are your caresses, my sister, my bride," the king exclaims. "How much better are your caresses than wine and the fragrance of your perfumes than any spice" (4:10). He encourages her advances; he desires that she feel comfortable and free with her demonstrations of affection.

Remember that during her first lonely visit to the palace, Shulamith spoke of her thirst for Solomon's kisses, which to her were "better than wine" (1:2). What she really craved was his undivided attention. Now she has it! And he very thoughtfully, very perceptively, reminds her of her earlier desire as they embrace. Wearing her most luscious and exotic fragrance, she smells irresistibly delicious to him. He is completely overwhelmed by her, as they begin to partake of love together.

The groom speaks again, his language becoming increasingly sensual, "Your lips, (my) bride, drip honey; Honey and milk are under your tongue" (4:11). Their kisses are exhilirating and sweet, eager and intimate. The image of milk and honey is used elsewhere in the Bible to describe the land of Canaan (see Exodus 3:8). Essentially, Solomon is telling Shulamith that she is his "promised land"—a source of joy and blessing, an incomparable gift from God.

But not only is she as precious as the land of milk and honey, she is to him "a garden locked . . . a spring locked, a fountain sealed" (4:12). He poetically compares her to a garden—not just any garden, but one that is locked, a sealed fountain or spring. This exquisite garden has been preserved for him. As her husband, he will be the first—

and only—to partake of the delights she offers. She has not been promiscuous, but protected, saved from the advances of other men so that she might guiltlessly enjoy the wholesome purity of the wedding night. He honors her for her chastity; she has kept herself for him.

Solomon continues speaking metaphorically of the "garden" of his bride. He praises her further, as he readies her for the consummation of their relationship. She is "a paradise of pomegranates with excellent fruit" (4:13). Her garden abounds with exquisite spices and lush vegetation: "henna blossoms with nard plants, nard and saffron, calamus and cinnamon, with all trees of frankincense, myrrh and aloes with all the choicest of spices" (4:13-14). She is invaluable to him, breathtakingly lovely and luscious.

He turns from speaking of her "garden" to comparing her to a fountain within its walls. She is, to him, "a garden fountain, a well of living water and streams flowing from Lebanon" (4:15). She refreshes him as she pours forth her love and allows it to wash over him. Tenderly he reminds her once more of her homeland. She is a priceless daughter of Lebanon. His desire is mounting . . . and so is hers.

"Awake, O north wind," cries the bride to the king, "And come, wind of the south. Blow upon my garden and let its spices flow forth. May my beloved come to his garden and eat its excellent fruit" (4:16). Shulamith refers to Solomon as the north and south wind, and requests that he come into his garden and partake of its delicacies. In other words, she invites him to consummate their marriage. Notice that she speaks of herself as "his" garden—she is fully willing to give herself to her lover. She is ready for this moment. He has prepared her by his consistent praise, sensitivity, consideration, and patience. Thanks to him, her sense of self-worth is solid; note that she speaks of her garden as a place of "excellent fruit."

Shulamith knows that her husband loves her for what she is, and does not think of her as simply a source of sexual gratification. The physical expression of their affection is not sordid but beautiful—the proper outgrowth of a fulfilled relationship, to which total commitment has been made. Locked in a mutual embrace, they drink wholeheartedly of their love and consummate their marriage.

Satisfied, the king pauses and reflects upon the wondrous passion they have just shared. "I have come into my garden, my sister, my bride" (5:1). He has accepted her gift of herself, and it has been pleasurable and rich. "I have gathered my myrrh with my balsam," he continues. "I have eaten my honeycomb with my honey. I have drunk my wine with my milk." It has been a thoroughly delicious experience.

Even after they have joined together in sexual love, Solomon remains a considerate lover. He lets his wife know that she is still a treasure to him. He uses the same words after they have made love that he employed previously to describe her "garden." He thus assures her that he feels the same way about her after the lovemaking as he did before they had known each other intimately.

I imagine that Solomon continues to hold Shulamith in his arms as he speaks these post-consummation words. Though satisfied, he still remains sensitive to her needs. The sexual responses of a woman are designed by God to build slowly. It takes time—and Solomon has been a patient lover, willing to stimulate his bride through words and caresses. Their first time of lovemaking has been exquisitely slow. He has not rushed, but has waited for her to be ready. He came unto her, remember, at her invitation. They communicate freely and fully throughout.

Just as a woman's desire mounts more slowly than a man's, neither does it wane immediately after consummation. Like Solomon, the sensitive husband will continue to hold his wife tenderly after they have made love. He will reassure her of his affection, speaking gently and romantically. Men, the physical should be more than a brief rendezvous on a Friday night. It should be a way of life. Our wife responds to commitment, consideration, patience, and planning.

An Eyewitness

What Solomon and Shulamith discover together on their wedding night is not vile or pornographic. It is not the stuff of magazine centerfolds and trashy literature glaring at us from bookstore shelves. It is a godly experience, involving two who have promised themselves to each other within the covenant of marriage. Sex is a meaningful part of a complete relationship, to be conducted with symphonic beauty and sheer sensitivity.

What is more, married love is witnessed with approval by a holy God. While the lovers remain entwined in the Song, a voice speaks in the palace bedroom, saying, "Eat, O loved ones; Drink and be drunk, O lovers" (5:1). While these might be the comments of an intruder, this is unlikely. No, the person who shares the intimacy of the king and his bride is the Lord Himself—the designer of all things, the creator of sexual love. And by these words, He gives His seal of approval to the their time of lovemaking. It is as if He is saying, "Rejoice in this pleasure, My children. It is My gift to you. Indulge freely and deeply."

With these words of divine sanction, the curtain falls on our scene of initial love. Yet the encounter between these two who waited for exactly the right moment offers several lessons for us to ponder.

LESSONS

Lesson number one: *Solomon is sensitive to the needs of his bride.* He builds her self-image and sense of security. He makes her feel valuable and loved and important.

Lesson two: *sexual love is more than simply physical.* Genuine lovers consider the spiritual, emotional, mental, and physical needs of their partner. Balance must be achieved, without undue emphasis on any one area. Neither husband nor wife should think of sex as mere physical gratification, nor should they spiritualize it to the degree that it is not pleasurable.

Lesson three explains itself: *the wedding night is especially joyful because of the purity which has preceded it.*

Four: *lovemaking involves free communication.* Solomon and Shulamith speak unreservedly to each other. We, too, mustn't let awkwardness or prudishness inhibit our verbal interaction during sex. That means the husband must be sensitive and considerate, encouraging his wife to express herself. It means that the wife must try to openly communicate, to talk to her husband. The result will be a more fulfilling and satisfying time together.

Five: *it takes time to make love.* Our bride and groom in the Song do not hurry through their experience. We can use discipline and planning to arrange for times of unrushed physical expression also. We can make "dates" with our spouse, packing the kids off to Grandma's or a friend's. We can reserve and prepare for periods alone with each other, just as we schedule appointments and meetings. Try it; you'll like it. And it's worth it!

Lesson six is perhaps the most important: *divine blessing is pronounced upon Solomon and Shulamith's relationship.* Sex between husband and wife is holy and God-ordained. When conducted with unselfishness and sensitivity, it is pleasing to the Lord. It doesn't defile, but rather exalts.

SHADOW AND REALITY

Just as Solomon, after the necessary delay, led the majestic procession into Shulamith's mountain village to claim his bride, so too will our bridegroom, Jesus Christ, return for all Christians someday. True love cannot be separated indefinitely. As the apostle Paul writes, one day we'll hear a shout like a trumpet, for . . .

> . . . the Lord Himself will descend from heaven with a shout, with the voice of the archangel, and with the trumpet of God; and the dead in Christ shall rise first. Then we who are alive and remain shall be caught up together in the clouds to meet the Lord in the air, and thus we shall always be with the Lord (1 Thessalonians 4:16-17 NASB).

This event, known in church history as the rapture, will occur at some point in the future. Perhaps it will be tomorrow that we who have received Christ as Savior will join Him in the clouds. It is His infinite love for us which makes this glorious hope possible. Always, let us remember the words of the hymn, "Jesus is coming again!"

Questions for Personal or Group Bible Study

1. In your opinion, why does Shulamith experience a fearful dream at the beginning of chapter 3 (verses 1-5)? If married, did you have a similar experience before your own wedding?

2. Describe the elaborate preparations Solomon had made so that he might come fetch his bride "in style" (see 3:6-11).

3. List some of the ways in which Solomon praises Shulamith as their wedding night commences (see 4:1-7).

4. When Solomon says to his bride, "With me from Lebanon, O bride, with me from Lebanon come. Journey from the . . . dens of lions and the mountains of leopards" (4:8), what is he really asking her to do?

5. Is the physical expression of love between man and wife sanctioned by God (see 5:1)?

6

Challenge

Song 5:2–7:1

The engaged couples whom I counsel usually appear to agree with me when I toss such comments as these in their direction: "There will be conflicts in your marriage. Although you have pledged your undying love, you are going to have problems with each other. You will disappoint each other. Occasionally, you may even question why you ever said 'I do,' in the first place, and you'll wonder if it might be easier to call it quits."

Typically, the sweethearts sitting in front of me nod their heads in reluctant acquiescence. Then they flash knowing looks and sly smiles at each other. You see, they don't really believe me. Inside they're thinking, not us! We're different! God put us together. We're so right for each other that we'll never say or do anything to seriously damage our relationship. We may have a few spats, sure, but nothing big. We're going to have a Christian marriage, after all!

Oh, but how often do these same pairs of young folks drag themselves back to my office within a few short years. Things aren't working out. Their marriage seems like a punishment for a crime perpetrated during a spell of temporary insanity. For committed Christians, the penalty is a life sentence, because divorce is (nearly) unthinkable. For many others, the time may seem tragically ripe to begin singing the words to John Denver's song, "Seasons of the Heart": "Love is why I came here in the first place; Love is now the reason I must go."

NOT RESOLVING MEANS NOT SOLVING

Most of the time the villain chomping at the tender roots of wedded love shows himself to be a monster indeed: the ogre of unresolved conflict. We're not talking about mere conflict, for differences of opinion between husbands and wives are only surprising if they don't exist. When two people get the "urge to merge" and travel the highway of matrimony, collisions are inevitable. Personalities clash, temperaments tussle, expectations soar far above reality, while irritating old habits suffer long, lingering deaths—making conflict a certainty. No, conflict itself is not the problem . . . unless it is allowed to remain unresolved or is dealt with unfairly. "Ay, there's the rub," as Hamlet would say (III.i). Improperly handled conflicts are catalysts for disaster. If differences are buried, they will eventually burst forth from their shallow graves to shower a couple with more dirt than can reasonably be shoveled away. Bitterness and resentment increase until a ground level explosion of emotion rocks the foundation of the marriage, making restoration of the relationship appear impossible.

Conflicts aren't solved by pretending they don't exist. Neither are they managed rightly if husband and wife turn into sparring partners who fight unfairly—jabbing below the belt with insults and sidestepping issues with blasts of ugly criticism. Fighting fairly means listening with an open mind and heart. And it's okay to feel angry during a heated discussion with one's spouse. The key lies in dealing correctly with that anger, keeping the hostility from roaring out of control and leveling one's "better half" with razor-sharp, soul-cutting remarks.

DISASTER BOUND

No book which I have read in recent years paints a more vivid and alarming picture of the dangers of improperly handled marital conflict than Pat and Jill Williamses' *Rekindled* (Revell, 1985). This painfully honest account of the Williamses' relationship exposes the tremendous danger of allowing differences to remain unresolved.

At first glance, the Williamses seemed perfectly matched—the epitome of a successful, loving Christian couple. Both were extremely talented. Pat, the highly-respected general manager of the Philadelphia 76ers basketball team, was also a successful author and popular conference and banquet speaker.

Jill, a former beauty queen, possessed a concert-quality voice which had entertained and ministered to thousands. Both were solidly devoted to Jesus Christ and, so they thought, to their marriage . . . at least in the beginning.

But after ten years of wrongs which had never been set right—a decade filled with genuine conflicts which had been shoved aside or smoothed over—their marriage teetered on the brink of destruction. One Sunday morning, a seemingly minor tiff escalated into a cold war lasting the rest of the day, until Pat confronted Jill and insisted she tell him what was wrong. Jill's reply astonished them both:

> "I just don't care anymore," she said, so quietly he almost couldn't hear her. Almost. "I hate this marriage. It's boring me to death." He heard that as if she'd screamed it in his ear, yet she spoke just above a whisper, staring at the floor. Pat leaned close to her face, realizing that she meant it, that her eyes and even her color signaled something in her he had never encountered. This wasn't something he could apologize away, something he could patch up with a babysitter and a dinner in Philly (Williams 1985, 20-21).

For perhaps the first time ever, Pat Williams truly listened to his wife, as Jill quietly reeled off a litany of complaints she had voiced through the years. The statements had been made often in the past, but he had never responded except with the intent to pacify, to submerge the conflict, to polish 'the rough edges while never touching the core. Now his strategy was backfiring in a devastating fashion. Jill sat before him emotionally dead, incapable of loving him or herself. And he was the one who had "killed" her. What were those complaints which thrust their marriage to the breaking point? Here is the list Jill recited on that awful day:

> *You don't really care about this marriage.*
>
> *Why should I try to be a good wife? You never notice anything anyway.*
>
> *We never do anything together unless it's something you want to do.*
>
> *You never share anything with me, your work, your Bible study, your dreams, your goals.*
>
> *Why can't you remember the little things, the special days, unless I circle them in red on the calendar?*
>
> *You talk to me like I'm a Philadelphia sportswriter.*
>
> *Couldn't you ever come home a little early just to be with me? Or come and pick me up and take me to the game instead of leaving me to find my own way there with friends?*
>
> *You never hold my hand anymore. You never touch me unless you want something more.*
>
> *You never say nice things to me in front of people.*
>
> *You're okay with the kids only after I've asked you five or six times.*
>
> *You never act as if my words are important. You never really listen. You either interrupt or don't let me talk at all when we're with other people.*
>
> *I don't want things. I want you. Don't give me crumbs. I want the real thing. You've never made a one hundred percent commitment to me. You've never really given me you* (Williams 1985, 21-22, italics in original).

Soon after she finished speaking, Jill left the room. She intended to stay married to Pat, but could make no promises of affection because there was nothing left to feel. She was emotionally desolate, numbed by years of vainly seeking the attention of her husband and encountering only unconscious indifference instead. Pat would have to pour every ounce of his energy into revitalizing a relationship which had been strained to its limits.

With God's help, the Williamses were able to rekindle the fires of love. Today their marriage is strong and vibrant. No longer do they ignore conflict, but rather deal with it openly and candidly—working as a team, with the Lord in charge. Their book is recommended reading for all who wish to "fight the good fight" in marriage and emerge with unity.

Yet even higher than *Rekindled* on my list of recommendations is a close reading of chapters 5 and 6 of the Song of Solomon. There the newlyweds face the first challenge in their marriage, as they deal with a conflict which cannot be allowed to go unresolved.

THE HONEYMOON'S OVER—SONG 5:2-6

> *Bride to Daughters of Jerusalem*
> 5:2 I was asleep but my heart was awake.
>   The sound of my beloved knocking,
>   "Open to me my sister, my darling, my dove, my
>   perfect one, for my hair is filled with dew; my
>   hair, with damp of the night."
>   3 I had put off my tunic; must I put it on again?
>   I had washed my feet; must I soil them again?
>   4 My beloved withdrew his hand from the door,
>   and my feelings were aroused for him.
>   5 I arose to open to my beloved
>   and my hand dripped with myrrh
>   and my fingers with flowing myrrh upon the
>   handle of the bolt.
>   6 I opened to my beloved, but my beloved had
>   turned and gone.
>   My soul had gone out to him when he spoke.
>   I sought him but did not find him;
>   I called out to him, but he did not answer me.
>   7 The watchmen who go about the city found me.
>   They struck me; they bruised me.
>   They took my shawl from upon me—those
>   guardians of the walls.

As we have been treated to glimpses of the love diary of Solomon and Shulamith, we have watched the sweetness of their courtship and the elegant ecstasy of their wedding night. The next scene in their drama occurs sometime later—days, weeks, maybe even months, after the honeymoon. It is the occasion of their first recorded conflict. You'll be disappointed if you expect fireworks and fisticuffs . . . but the disagreement is there nonetheless. Allow me to set the stage.

The episode opens in Shulamith's chambers at the palace. She has prepared herself for bed and is drifting off to sleep. Solomon has evidently been out of town on some sort of business trip but has managed to arrange his schedule so that he might return to Jerusalem earlier than anticipated. While Shulamith does not expect her husband, he has missed her terribly and longs to be with her again.

She relates her version of the ensuing incident to the women of the court. "I was asleep but my heart was awake," Shulamith recalls (5:2). From the doorway, Solomon's gentle knocks can be heard, rousing her from semi-consciousness. Then comes his voice, calling to her tenderly.

"Open to me my sister, my darling, my dove, my perfect one, for my hair is filled with dew; my hair, with damp of the night," he asks of her. Standing outside the locked bedroom door, his hair dripping with the chill wetness of the night, the king waits for his wife's reply. They have been apart much too long and he yearns to be with his beloved bride! Surely his "darling," his "dove," his "perfect one," will bound to the door, throw it open, and leap into his arms with eager expectation.

But not so. "I had put off my tunic; must I put it on again?" asks Shulamith. "I had washed my feet; must I soil them again?" (5:3). Instead of ecstasy, Solomon is greeted with indifference. Shulamith has already changed into her nightgown. She has taken her bath. She is ready to retire—in fact she has been half-asleep—and so Solomon's hopeful yet untimely approach is met only with a yawn and excuses. She might as well have said, "Not tonight, dear. I'm too tired."

What about that? The king of all Israel has especially arranged his schedule so that he can be home with his bride, and she refuses even to crawl out of bed and tiptoe across the room to unlatch the door for him! What a crushing blow to his male ego!

A Fox Begins to Nibble

The attitude of disinterest displayed here by Shulamith toward her husband could be hazardous to the health of their marriage. We recall that earlier Solomon has cautioned her to beware of the "little foxes," the little dangers, which must not be permitted to creep into their relationship (see 2:15). If allowed to gnaw at their marriage, the "fox" of apathy pictured in chapter 5 could do considerable damage. Indifference wounds pride and breeds bitterness, resentment, and eventually, contempt. In any form, it is bad. But if a wife is sexually indifferent toward her husband, as Shulamith is in this instance, the consequences can be severe.

In *Maximum Marriage,* Tim Timmons includes a humorous letter written by a frustrated husband to his frustrating wife. Hopefully the contents will be laughable, but the message may strike a bit too close to home for many of us, I fear.

To My Loving Wife,

During the past year I have tried to make love to you 365 times. I have succeeded only thirty-six times; this is an average of once every ten days. The following is a list of the reasons why I did not succeed more often: It was too late, too early, too hot, or too cold. It would waken the children, the company in the next room, or the neighbors whose windows were open. You were too full; or you had a headache, backache, toothache, or the giggles. You pretended to be asleep or were not in the mood. You had on your mudpack. You watched the late TV show; I watched the late TV show; or the baby was crying.

During the times I did succeed the activity was not entirely satisfactory for a variety of reasons. Six times you chewed gum the whole time; on occasion you watched TV the whole time. Often you told me to hurry up and get it over with. A few times I tried to waken you to tell you we were through; and one time I was afraid I had hurt you for I felt you move.

Honey, it's no wonder I drink too much.

YOUR LOVING HUSBAND
(Timmons 1976, 114)

Ladies, if I may speak plainly, it is so very important to your husband that you be sexually responsive. There are many others out there who undoubtedly find your man attractive and would be willing to satisfy him physically. You expose him to temptation and senseless frustration if you persist in sexual indifference or repeatedly resist his overtures (again, the reader is directed to Dr. James Dobson's *What Wives Wish Their Husbands Knew about Women*, Tyndale, 1975). If the romance in your marriage has fizzled like that of the "Loving Wife" in the letter above, please confess the situation to the Lord and ask that He help you change things. After all, He is the designer of sexual intimacy. And I urge you to take to heart this choice advice concerning sex in marriage, given by the apostle Paul to the Corinthian Christians: "Stop depriving one another, except by agreement for a time that you may devote yourselves to prayer, and come together again lest Satan tempt you because of your lack of self-control" (1 Corinthians 7:5 NASB).

In fairness, while a wife's unresponsiveness may mortally wound a marriage, it must be pointed out that many women become sexually indifferent because of the man they live with. If a husband is hurried, anxious to physically please only himself—if he is inconsiderate or even abusive—who can fault his wife if she is less than eager for intimacy?

Working out the sexual relationship so that it is mutually satisfying is one of the biggest, albeit one of the most potentially pleasurable, tasks of any pair of newlyweds. It is a delicate assignment which should literally last a lifetime, too. Song of Solomon 5-6 records for us merely the first challenge confronting the king and his bride in this bittersweet area.

WHO'S TO BLESS AND WHO'S TO BLAME?

If we must place the blame for this first conflict, it can be argued that the fault is largely Shulamith's. Solomon has already shown himself to be a thoughtful, tender, and patient lover—concerned with pleasing his wife (see Song 4). As we picture him standing vainly outside the door to his bride's chamber in Song 5, let us also remember that he has carefully organized his pressing schedule so that they might have time alone. In rejecting him, she levels a shot of ingratitude at him which knocks the wind right out of his sails. Yet we mustn't forget that she is young and that they both have much to learn about each other. Hers is a natural, very understandable, very human, mistake.

IS IT TOO LATE TO SAY I'M SORRY?

It is a mistake which Shulamith quickly comes to regret. Apparently, Solomon has opened her bedroom door ever so slightly—as far, perhaps, as the chain will allow. Seeing that entry is impossible, he gently closes it again.

"My beloved withdrew his hand from the door," recalls Shulamith in verse 4, "and my feelings were aroused for him." Suddenly she realizes she'd like to see him after all. Quickly she throws off the covers and gets up from the bed. She strides to the door and reaches for the latch, unfastening the chain.

"I arose to open to my beloved," Shulamith continues reporting to the palace women, "and my hand dripped with myrrh and my fingers with flowing myrrh upon the handles of the bolt. I opened to my beloved, but my beloved had turned and gone" (5:5-6). She pushes open the bedroom door, but it is too late; Solomon is not to be seen. Instead of her lover, she finds only a vial of the rich perfume—the myrrh—which he has left. He must have hung a container of her favorite fragrance upon the handle of her door. He has likely purchased this gift for her while away; it is a little item to tangibly tell her how much he has missed her.

We men can learn a great deal from Solomon's response to the challenge of his wife's indifference. The king could have fumed with rage at her reluctance. He could easily have forced his way into the room, ordering his guards to bash down the door if necessary. At the very least he could have stalked off heatedly, keeping his gift for a time when she'd be more receptive. Instead, Solomon graciously leaves the present of perfume and departs to go about his business. He knows that Shulamith must be tired, exhausted from a difficult day. It is the time for him to exercise self-discipline. True love such as his is sensitive to the needs of the one loved.

"My soul had gone out to him when he spoke," reflects Shulamith further (5:6). Desire reawakens to replace the earlier hesitation. Disappointed at finding her lover gone, Shulamith reacts properly. Rather than taking a chance that the emotional wound she has inflicted upon him will fester, she springs into action. She slips on her clothes and sets out to locate her man. She first searches the palace hallways. Alas, it is to no avail.

"I sought him but did not find him; I called out to him, but he did not answer me," she mourns to the women of the court (5:6). Solomon is nowhere to be found. Shulamith's belated attempt to seize the moment leaves her grasping only empty handfuls of air.

The situation goes from bad to worse, degenerating into a royal snafu, the likes of which Shulamith couldn't have anticipated in her worst dreams. After failing to track down her husband in the palace, she steps out into the city streets. There she is accosted by the city police, the "watchmen," who are out on patrol. They treat her roughly.

"They struck me; they bruised me. They took my shawl from upon me," Shulamith bitterly tells the court ladies, sarcastically describing her captors as "these guardians of the walls" (5:7).

Yet probably worse than any of this harrassment is the fact that she has not been able to find Solomon. She longs to see him, to touch him, to beg his forgiveness. Bruised and battered, furious with the local policemen, frantically missing her man, grief-stricken over her earlier error, Shulamith's emotions surely churn and threaten to boil over in tearful despair. Where is her lover?

HE IS EVERYTHING TO ME—SONG 5:8-16

> *Bride to Daughters of Jerusalem*
> 5:8 I adjure you, O daughters of Jerusalem,
>   if you find my beloved—as to what you will
>   tell him—
>   (tell him) that I am faint with love.
> *Daughters of Jerusalem to Bride*
>   9 What is your beloved more than another lover,
>   O fairest among women?
>   What is your beloved more than another lover,
>   that you so adjure us?
> *Bride to Daughters of Jerusalem*
>   10 My beloved is dazzlingly ruddy,
>   distinguished among ten thousand.
>   11 His head is pure gold;
>   His locks, palm leaves, black as a raven.
>   12 His eyes are like doves beside streams of water,
>   bathed in milk and reposed in their setting.
>   13 His cheeks are a bed of balsam, a raised bed of
>   spices.
>   His lips are lilies, dripping with liquid myrrh.
>   14 His hands are cylinders of gold set with jewels.
>   His abdomen is a plate of ivory covered with
>   sapphires.

15 His legs are alabaster pillars set upon pedestals
   of fine gold.
   His appearance is like Lebanon, choice as the
   cedars.
16 His mouth is sweetness,
   And all of him is wonderful.
   This is my beloved and this is my friend,
   O daughters of Jerusalem.

At length, Shulamith concludes her account of the night's misadventures and turns to the women of the palace, imploring them to assist her in her search for Solomon. "I adjure you, O daughters of Jerusalem, if you find my beloved . . . (tell him) that I am faint with love," she pleads (5:8). Since she cannot locate Solomon herself, she at least wants him to know that she is lovesick for his presence. She regrets her previous reluctance and craves his company.

But, why? "What is your beloved more than another lover, O fairest among women?" ask the court ladies. "What is your beloved more than another lover, that so you adjure us?" (5:9). In other words, the palace pretties want to know what makes Solomon so great. Why is Shulamith's heart aching over his absence? (Incidentally, the fact that the court women cannot speak intimately of the king suggests strongly that he has remained faithful to his wife and has not strayed into their arms.)

What makes Solomon so terrific? Just look at what Shulamith has to say in return about her man. Have his words of praise been lost on her? Has he been wasting syllables in showering her with the many compliments we've seen in previous chapters (see 4:1-7)? Not at all. Shulamith responds to her husband's consistent praise and heartfelt appreciation. She may have made a mistake earlier this evening, but she is willing to search him out, fall at his feet, and beg his forgiveness. In the meantime, she is prepared to extol his virtues in front of a flock of females—praising her man from head to toe! How highly she regards this lover who has diligently and sensitively worked to build her self-image!

A SIGHT TO BEHOLD

"My beloved is dazzlingly ruddy," says Shulamith to the women of the court (5:10). He is handsome; his flushed face glows with health and vitality. He is a man among men—"distinguished among ten thousand" (5:10)—the first to be spotted in even a vast crowd. Notice that the bride's words echo the compliments Solomon has already paid her. Remember that he has likened her to "a mare among the chariots of Pharaoh" (1:9) and he has also assured her that, compared to other young women, she is as "a lily among thorns" (2:2). Now she responds in kind.

Shulamith continues speaking of her lover. "His head is pure gold; His locks, palm leaves, black as a raven," she muses. The deep, rich bronze of his tanned face reminds her of burnished gold. Raven-black hair thickly tops his handsome head, much as a cluster of palm leaves adorns that familiar and stately tree. To her, he is incredibly attractive!

"His eyes," says Shulamith of Solomon, "are like doves beside streams of water, bathed in milk and reposed in their setting" (5:12). The king's eyes are clear, soft, and gentle. The portion surrounding each dark pupil is the milky white tint of health. Twice before, Solomon has spoken of the clarity, the beauty, the dove-like quality of Shulamith's eyes (see 1:15, 4:1). Now she describes his in the same manner, and we sense that both lovers can look directly and plainly into each other's eyes and speak of their affection. There is no inhibition, no hesitancy, no lingering doubt, no creeping dishonesty nor hidden impurity to prevent such candid contact.

AND A DELIGHT TO BE NEAR

Not only are Solomon's eyes wonderful but, as Shulamith continues her description, "His cheeks are a bed of balsam, a raised bed of spices. His lips are lilies, dripping with liquid myrrh. His hands are cylinders of gold set with jewels" (5:13-14). In other words, Solomon takes care of his appearance, even after he has won his bride. His cheeks aren't rough, but soothing, as fragrant as a "raised bed of spices." He showers, grooms his beard, and slaps on cologne before coming to see her—there's nothing bristly, scratchy, or unappealing about him! His lips are as soft as lilies and as sweet to the taste and smell as perfume. His hands aren't calloused either but are well-manicured, smooth to the touch, slick as polished bars of gold. He cares about being physically appealing to his wife.

I wonder how many of us go to such trouble when we're ready to spend time with our spouse. Certainly during the days of courtship, we took extra pains with our appearance. If you don't remember, try watching your teenagers prepare for a big date. Your daughter will spend hours locked in the bathroom with her shampoo, conditioner, blow dryer, curling iron, nail polish, cosmetics and creams. She'll wash and brush and shine and fuss till she's ready to stun. Then she'll fly to the bedroom and throw on and off almost every item of clothing in her closet until she hits just the right combination.

And your teenaged son—a big date transforms the kid who at age nine avoided showers like drops of acid rain, into a stranger who steams up the bathroom for forty-five minutes. He emerges sporting styled hair and one-quarter of a bottle of extravagantly-priced cologne. With shirt and slacks neatly pressed, he departs to pick up his girl, leaving his astonished parents in the dust.

Do you still go to the same trouble now that you are married? It is important to present ourselves to our husband or wife at our very best, especially when we have lovemaking in mind! Evidently Solomon does exactly that.

What is more, he fights the battle of the bulge, also! "His abdomen is a plate of ivory covered with sapphires," says Shulamith to the women of the court. Solomon must exercise and watch his eating habits—how else can his midsection be as firm as a slab of ivory? And his legs are muscular and solid and strong: "alabaster pillars set upon pedestals of fine gold," according to his wife (5:15).

In fact, the king is grand and powerful and utterly breathtaking to his woman. "His appearance is like Lebanon, choice as the cedars," she states in verse 15, comparing her beloved to the place most precious to her in all the world, her native land. Often as a young girl she had gazed with awe upon the towering cedars and majestic mountains of her country. Now Solomon, her husband and lover, evokes the same reaction from her. He overwhelms her and, as she speaks of him, her enthusiasm bubbles up and spills over in words of heartfelt adoration.

A LOVER . . . AND A FRIEND

"His mouth is sweetness, And all of him is wonderful," Shulamith next exclaims of her man (5:16). Solomon does not speak roughly or crossly to her; his words are kind and gentle and sweet. To her way of thinking, all of him is wonderful—not just his physique but his personality. He is compassionate, considerate, and charming.

Shulamith concludes her description of Solomon with these words: "This is my beloved and this is my friend, O daughters of Jerusalem" (5:16). What about that? He is her friend, her very best friend. Nowhere in her speech does Shulamith boast of her husband's virility, his aggressiveness, his sexual prowess. Rather, she applauds his kindness, his thoughtfulness, his sensitivity. She caps a totally flattering portrait with the ultimate compliment of all, calling Solomon her "friend." And your friendship, men, is what your wife wants from you more than anything else!

FINDING HIM AGAIN—SONG 6:1–7:1

Daughters of Jerusalem to Bride
6:1 Where has your beloved gone, O fairest among women?

Where has your beloved turned, that we may
seek him with you?

Bride to Daughters of Jerusalem

2   My beloved has gone to his garden, to beds of
balsam,
to pasture his flock among the gardens
and to gather lilies.

3   I am my beloved's and my beloved is mine—the
one who pastures his flock among the lilies.

King to Bride

4   Fair you are, my darling, as Tirzah,
lovely as Jerusalem,
awe-inspiring as bannered hosts.

5   (Turn you eyes from me for they arouse me.)
Your hair is like a flock of goats which descend
from Gilead.

6   Your teeth are like a flock of young lambs,
which have come up from the washing,
all of which are paired,
and not one among them is alone.

7   Your temples are like a slice of a pomegranate
behind your veil.

8   There are sixty queens and eighty concubines
and maidens without number;

9   (But) unique is she—my dove, my perfect one;
unique is she to her mother;
pure is she to the one who bore her.
The daughters saw her and called her blessed;
The queens and concubines praised her,

10 "Who is this looking forth like the dawn,
fair as the moon,
pure as the sun,
awesome as an army with banners?"

Bride in soliloquy

11 To the garden of nut trees I had gone down
to see the fresh shoots of the ravine,
to see whether the vine had budded or the
pomegranates had bloomed.

12 Before I was aware, my soul set me among the
    chariots of my people, a prince.
Daughters of Jerusalem to Bride
13 Return, return O Shulamith;
    Return, return, that we may gaze upon you.
King to Daughters of Jerusalem
7:1 How you gaze upon Shulamith;
    as at a dance of Mahanaim!

As Shulamith wraps up her exuberant description of
Solomon, she desires more than ever to find him. Apparently the women of the court are ready to beat down the
bushes in search of him too because they cry, "Where has
your beloved gone, O fairest among women? Where has
your beloved turned, that we may seek him with you?"
(6:1). In other words, "C'mon Shulamith, let's go get him!
Men like that don't grow on trees! We can't afford to let this
one get away!"

Where, O Where, Can He Be?

Flushed with excitement, the wheels start turning in
Shulamith's mind. Where would her lover go to be alone, to
think things over? Suddenly, she remembers!

"My beloved has gone to his garden, to beds of balsam,
to pasture his flock among the gardens and to gather lilies," she says (6:2). She knows him well enough to finally
figure out where he might be. He is probably walking in
the midst of his garden, the site where he keeps what is
perhaps a small flock of favorite sheep. Maybe he is picking
flowers as he reflects on ways to settle the conflict which
has cropped up earlier in the evening. Perhaps he waits
there for her because it is their special place . . . and he
knows that she will eventually come.

Shulamith utters much the same words of total commitment she voiced after she originally accepted Solomon's
proposal of marriage: "I am my beloved's and my beloved
is mine" (6:3, see also 2:16). It is as if she is recommitting

herself to this man, this lover, this gentle shepherd "who pastures his flocks among the lilies" (6:3). And off she goes to find him.

WILL HE BE ANGRY. . . WILL HE BE SAD?

It will be interesting to see how Solomon receives his wife. After all, Shulamith's indifference could well have demolished his masculine pride. When a challenge such as this arises in a relationship, some men seethe with anger and hurt, and flatly refuse to communicate. The new game is all looks and no language; it's the "silent treatment," but if looks could kill . . . .

Then comes the pouting stage: "All right, if that's the way you want it—you sleep on your side of the bed and I'll stay on mine, and thank goodness our mattress is king-sized!" And the angry lovers roll over with cold hearts and slow sighs much like air escaping a balloon. When the ice thaws a bit and communication is loosed—watch out! Hostility pours out accusations marked by such phrases as: "You never do this!" "You always do that!"—invectives guaranteed to draw blood. Have you been there? I have, and the length of the whole confrontation usually signals the level of maturity of the opponents: the longer the fight, the more immature the fighters. Is this how Solomon responds to Shulamith's approach?

It is not. Remember that she compares him to a gentle shepherd (6:2-3). Like any shepherd caring lovingly for his flock, he will guide their conflict to a peaceful and proper resolution.

"Fair you are, my darling, as Tirzah, lovely as Jerusalem, awe-inspiring as bannered hosts," Solomon tells Shulamith as she comes near to him (6:4). Imagine that! His first comment to her after she has failed to respond to him physically is a sincere compliment! He doesn't greet her with bitter remarks or wrathful accusations. He realizes that she is probably a bit nervous, a little shaky, as she approaches. She is not totally sure what to expect from him. After all, this has been their first fight (as far as we know). She's ready to apologize but she is somewhat hesitant to speak.

So he tells her that she is lovely. I imagine Shulamith breathes a sigh of relief at hearing such words of high praise. Not only is she as attractive to Solomon as the city of Tirzah, she is as beautiful to behold as Jerusalem itself! To understand that compliment fully, one must realize that to Solomon Jerusalem is the loveliest city in the world. Brenda Lesley Segal's book about Masada is called *The Tenth Measure* for this very reason. As Segal's characters reveal, it was said that in all the world, nine measures of beauty existed, but the tenth measure of beauty was found entirely within the city of Jerusalem. Thus, in likening Shulamith to Jerusalem, Solomon means that she is the loveliest woman of them all. Even after her mistake, she remains to him, "a lily among thorns" (2:2) when compared to other ladies.

During their days of courtship, Shulamith had mused of the king, "his banner over me is love" (2:4). Now Solomon tells her that she is "awe-inspiring as bannered hosts" (6:4). She takes his breath away, inviting such respect, reverence, and appreciation as thousands of mighty warriors marching in formation might enkindle in the heart of a military man.

FIRST, LET'S WORK THIS OUT

She thrills him so that he begs her, "Turn your eyes from me for they arouse me" (6:5). Why does he ask that she look away? The answer illustrates the wisdom of the king. Solomon refuses to commit the error of so many men—that is, to assume that a session of lovemaking will cure the cause of a conflict. Trying to settle a disagreement by offering the old cliche, "Let's kiss and make up," is like saying to a child who has broken his arm, "Let me kiss it and make it better." Indeed, more than one woman has filed for divorce the morning after having sex with her husband. And recall, if you will, that Shulamith has told the ladies of the court that she is "faint with love" for Solomon (5:8). She would probably like him to make love to her—and this desire he evidently detects.

She gazes at him with lovesick eyes as she approaches him in the garden; her mere glance stirs him physically. But wise lover that he is, the king recognizes the fact that their problems must be worked out before sex can be truly satisfying. Forgiveness must first be given and received.

Solomon also realizes that he must be sensitive to the needs of his wife. In his book *Solomon on Sex*, Jody Dillow suggests that two verses from the New Testament book of 1 Peter are especially applicable here. In 1 Peter 3:7, husbands are commanded to live with their wife "in an understanding way" (NASB). That section of the verse might be expanded this way: "Husbands, live with your wife in a way that is based on a personal evaluation of her needs." Suggestions as to how to go about living with one's wife (or husband) in "an understanding way" are found in 1 Peter 3:9, where the apostle writes that we should not be "returning evil for evil, or insult for insult, but giving a blessing instead" (NASB). This is essentially what Solomon does in chapter 6 of his Song (Dillow 1977, 120).

The king has been, so-to-speak, slapped in the face by his wife's lack of interest. Instead of insulting her in return, he offers his forgiveness by speaking words of blessing and appreciation. Many of the statements he makes are strikingly similar to the ones he uttered on their wedding night. It is as if he is assuring her that his affections have not changed. His love is not based on what she does but on what she is.

I'll Love You If . . .

Far too frequently husbands and wives may lay the foundation of their love for each other upon conditional expectations of performance. That is like erecting a house upon shifting, sandy soil; it is terribly unstable ground on which to build. Unconsciously spouses often communicate such attitudes as these to each other: "I'll love you as long as you take care of the kids . . . take care of the house . . . take care of me. You can stick around as long as your performance is up to snuff and you please me." Not so with Solomon.

Instead, the king's attachment to Shulamith is unconditional—and as intense as it was on the day they were married. Using very much the same words he spoke on their wedding night, he compliments her hair, her smile, and her rosy countenance (6:5-7, see also 4:1-3).

And again he assures her that she is a woman above all women. "There are sixty queens and eighty concubines and maidens without number," says Solomon to his bride. "(But) unique is she—my dove, my perfect one; unique is she to her mother; pure is she to the one who bore her" (6:8-9). She is peerless and flawless. Just because she has met his advances with apathy has not changed his opinion of her. Solomon has made room in their relationship for failure. How critical it is in a deepening bond to anticipate and make allowances for times like these.

Indeed, according to Solomon, even other women recognize the matchless virtue and noble beauty of his wife. In his words:

> The daughters saw her and called her blessed;
> The queens and concubines praised her,
>   "Who is this looking forth like the dawn,
>   fair as the moon,
>   pure as the sun,
>   awesome as an army with banners?" (6:9-10).

Apparently Shulamith has rejoined Solomon. Perhaps they are walking to where the women of the court are waiting. Maybe they are riding in his chariot, heading back to the palace. Possibly the daughters of Jerusalem spy them and call out the remarks reprinted above. These Solomon hears and repeats for Shulamith's benefit. He is sensitive to seize any opportunity to make her feel good about herself. Obviously, the conflict is over. He has offered his forgiveness and she has accepted it. They are together again.

THE THREE H'S

Before Shulamith came to him in the garden, Solomon had some choices to make as to how he would handle the challenge which had arisen in their marriage. Today husbands and wives face essentially the same choices when the winds of conflict howl and threaten to topple their closeness. I call these choices the three H's.

The first option in the midst of marital challenge is to *hide*. Hiding occurs when the problem is not dealt with, but buried. It is when resentment is kept within, the wounded party submerging hurt feelings rather than laying them bare before the one who has inflicted the injury. Hiding may also involve physically running away from the trouble. I do not mean walking away from a disagreement in order to cool off. I mean leaving the situation—running home to Mother, out to a bar, into the arms of another—in order to escape the hassle of hashing out the difficulties. In the long run, hidden problems have a way of making themselves ominously evident, springing up eventually with crushing consequences.

Another option when facing a challenge in marriage is to *hurl*. Get behind your own little wall and let your mate have it with every verbal rock you can throw. You have a memory like an elephant—use it to dredge up each past indiscretion, failure, or error and blast away at your spouse. Let 'em have it! You'll feel so good if you do . . . while you're firing, that is. After the smoke clears, you'll be left with a injured party on your hands and a relationship which might be damaged beyond repair. The hurtful comments you hurl forth cannot be retrieved and the memory of them will linger in your spouse's mind long after the fight is finished.

The third choice one can make when facing a marital conflict is to determine to *help* the situation. That means responding as Solomon did: with kind words and blessings. It means talking over the issues, digging to the root of the problem, seeking God's wisdom in His Word. Let your temper subside first. Determine to be unmoved in your devotion and commitment to your spouse. Do whatever you can to unselfishly help the situation. Believe me, helping beats hiding or hurling every time! And when constructive change comes from conflict, the relationship has deepened and growth has taken place.

THROUGH HER EYES

Solomon could easily slice Shulamith to pieces emotionally with sharp words of rebuke and reproach. But he doesn't, even though it would be the natural thing to do. He does the supernatural thing instead, responding with compassion and charity to her request for forgiveness. How does she look at the incident in the garden? The closing words of Song of Solomon 6 give us a clue.

"To the garden of nut trees I had gone down," Shulamith recalls of her trip to Solomon's garden, "to see the fresh shoots of the ravine, to see whether the vine had budded or the pomegranates had bloomed" (6:11). She has been looking for signs of spring—vital signs that their love can be renewed, that it can bloom afresh once again, that although she has wronged her man, he will still desire her. Has she slain the fox of apathy in time, before it has completely spoiled the vineyard of their love?

What does she find at her destination? "Before I was aware, my soul set me among the chariots of my people, a prince," she sighs (6:12). In the garden of forgiveness she finds a prince among men who is willing to freely accept her apology. Solomon still loves her with his whole heart, mind, and soul. His commitment to her has been untouched by the winds of adversity which have blown. She is sheltered and safe in the cleft of his unconditional love for her.

Besides, making up isn't too bad, either! The text suggests that perhaps Solomon sweeps his bride into his chariot and they drive off together in a whirlwind of majesty. It reminds me of a romantic movie where the hero and heroine ride off into the sunset to live happily ever after.

"Return, return O Shulamith," the women of the court evidently called after them, "Return, return, that we may gaze upon you" (6:13). No doubt Shulamith is glowing with the reflected love of her man—she is a sight to behold! As the king replies to the gawking palace crowd, possibly calling back to them as his chariot speeds away, "How you gaze at Shulamith as at a dance of Mahanaim!" (7:1). In other words, "Of course you're looking upon my dazzling bride! She is worthy of being the center of attention!"

And thanks to her lover, she is.

LESSONS

This episode of challenge in the life of the king and the country girl become queen offers us many lessons to consider. Here are a few.

Lesson one: *every marriage experiences times of adjustment.* They are natural occurrences; expect them.

Two: *it is possible to overcome such adjustments with real victory.* Solomon and Shulamith show us how to do just that, as they cool off and then begin to communicate, and as Solomon offers his love unconditionally.

Lesson three: *the unwillingness to forgive and forget past wrongs can spoil a relationship.* Men and women have difficulty leaving the past where it belongs: behind them. Each time a previous failure is thrown up to one's spouse, the evidence is clear that there has been no forgiving, and certainly no forgetting. Just the other day I counseled a couple in severe difficulty. The husband is simply unwilling to accept his wife's apology for a very personal injury. Their relationship is sinking fast but still has the potential to be fantastic if only he can allow himself to forgive her.

Lesson four: *forgiveness must be granted generously . . . and it must be received graciously.* Not only does Solomon accept Shulamith's apology, but she accepts his forgiveness.

Five: *true love in conflict remains sensitive to needs.*

Solomon recognized that Shulamith's self-image had to be bolstered and that she needed reassurrance that their marriage was secure. He didn't say anything to damage her self-esteem or to cause her to question his love for her. He chose his words carefully and well.

Lesson six: *it is better to respond to conflict than to react to it.* As Shulamith approached him in the garden, Solomon could have reacted with anger and resentment. Instead he responded with kind words and a heartfelt desire to mend the rift.

Lesson seven: *when faced with a marital challenge, favorably recalling the wedding night is a good thing to do.* Remind yourself—and your spouse—of the passion, the joy, and the promise. Say, "No matter what happens, I'll never stop loving you," and mean it!

Eight: *conflict provides us with the opportunity to either widen a chasm or to develop greater closeness.* It can split you and your mate apart, or it can be the catalyst to cause you to draw closer together.

Nine: one way that husbands and wives grow closer is through change. Indeed, *change often results in closeness.* I'm not talking about attempts to change each other. Instead, as you become different yourself—altering bad habits, becoming more considerate or responsive—your mate will notice the results. You'll be assuring your spouse that your marriage is important, more than worth whatever effort is necessary.

Lesson ten: *the closer our expectations are to reality, the happier we're going to be.* Solomon would have relished a joyous reunion with his wife after his business trip, but when she did not respond as he would have liked, he didn't allow himself to wallow in bitterness and misery. He faced the reality of the situation: she was probably tired and there would be other occasions for intimacy. And was he ever right, as we'll see in the final chapters of his Song!

ANOTHER HAPPY ENDING

It is essential to the survival of a marriage that the challenges of the relationship be properly met. As we discussed earlier in this chapter, the marriage of Pat and Jill Williams very nearly crashed against the rocks of unresolved conflicts which had piled up during their years together. Two years after the fateful Sunday of confrontation, Jill could write this note to her husband, with whom she had once again fallen in love. On the day during which the Williamses legalized their adoption of two Korean orphans—a dream of Jill's which had long been ignored—Pat found this message from his wife:

> *Dear Pat,*
> *I love you so much for your response to that darkest hour two years ago today. And a large part of that response encompasses two Oriental dolls sleeping upstairs tonight. That you would share your name, life, and love with them is beyond their understanding . . . that you would share your name, life, love, and your-self with me is truly my dream come true. There aren't enough words to express my love and devotion to you—I am the most blessed of all women.*
>
> *Love, Jill*
> (Williams 1985, 154,
> italics in original)

LOVE, NO MATTER WHAT

As I read over this account of the first challenge to hit the marriage of Solomon and Shulamith, I reflect upon the beauty of his unconditional love for her. He does not withdraw his affection because she fails to measure up. He loves her anyway, despite her indifference. That is the way Christ deals with us, too. No matter how dismally we perform, He accepts us. He loves us anyway!

Christ's love is total, encompassing even those who never come to know Him as personal Savior. Don't misunderstand—those who fail to believe that Jesus paid the price for their own sins will never rest in eternity with Him (John 14:6). But as Christ loves Christians, so also He loves non-Christians. It is the lost He died to save (Romans 5:8).

The Word of God contains many examples of how Jesus continued to love, no matter what. In the upper room, the Lord washed the feet of Judas Iscariot, although He knew that only hours later Judas would betray Him (see John 13:2-5). "They hated Me without a cause," Christ was to say that same evening, when speaking of those in the world (John 15:25 NASB). How amazing that He was willing to die for men and women who unjustly despised Him! And Luke 23:34 records the words Jesus uttered upon Calvary, after the nails pinning Him to the cross had pierced His flesh and while the Roman soldiers guarding Him gambled for His robes: "Father forgive them; for they do not know what they are doing" (NASB).

Christ's affection—that agape love so amazing, so divine—overshadows the sinfulness of humanity. His love for us is total, unconditional, eternal. It doesn't diminish as we fail Him.

Can we say the same thing about our love for those around us? Don't we sometimes tend to make a judgment of our Christian brothers and sisters based on their performance? We love them as long as they love us? We scratch their backs as long as they scratch ours? Then the day inevitably comes when they disappoint us in some way, and we're finished with them! We sever the ties that are supposed to bind. We can be so quick to write people off, to kill any potential for future closeness by hoisting flags of perfectionism. We must not let such behavior characterize our relationships with others . . . and certainly our responses toward our husband or wife shouldn't be dictated by whether or not their performance pleases us!

In Song of Solomon 5 and 6, the king makes it clear that an act of physical indifference will not affect his love for his wife. Shulamith means more to him than that. And because they have handled the challenge properly, the injury will be quickly forgotten, while the relationship will endure. As we shall see, the newlyweds rise above the wrong to experience even greater intimacy as the years go by.

Questions for Personal or Group Study

1. How does Shulamith respond when she hears Solomon's unexpected knock at her door (see 5:2-6)? What does Solomon do when she fails to answer his call (see 5:4-6)?

2. List some of the compliments Shulamith pays Solomon as she describes him to the women of the court (see 5:10-16). In your opinion, which of these is the highest compliment of all? Explain.

3. Shulamith realizes that Solomon has probably gone to walk in his garden; she seeks him there. With what words does he greet her (6:4)? What does his response to her tell us about his compassion and sensitivity to her needs?

4. Why does the king instruct Shulamith not to look at him in Song 6:5?

5. What phrases, in chapter 6, does Solomon use to describe Shulamith which remind us of words he had spoken on their wedding night (see 6:5-7; see also 4:1-7)?

6. How, in your opinion, do we know that their conflict has been resolved at the close of chapter 6? Explain.

7

Communion

Song 7:1–8:14

The rough-hewn man sitting before me was in his sixties. He had been a hard-nosed businessman for forty years—always ready to make a deal, as long as it was to his advantage. His name was included on the rolls of the local church which he had attended most of his life, yet from our conversation I doubted that he knew the Lord as his Savior. Brusquely he answered my questions and shot me a few himself. His crustiness softened, however, as soon as we began to speak of his marriage.

His wife was a radiant Christian lady. Her face literally shone, despite the fact that she had been confined to a wheelchair for years. Although her husband was evidently not a God-fearing man, he did love her intensely; their marriage was happy. It was, perhaps, the area of his life of which this man was the most proud.

"My wife," he said to me, "is the most wonderful woman who has ever lived. It has been my privilege to keep company with her for nearly forty years."

Basking in the glow of his obvious affection, the wife looked at me and, indicating her husband, responded with these words. "There sits the finest man that ever walked this earth."

I've found it's best not to argue with a woman in love. But to agree that this gruff, tough man was the finest male to ever walk the earth was a little too much for me to swallow. To my way of thinking, the fellow had more than his share of faults. But in his wife's mind and heart, he was the best thing that had ever happened to her.

So I began to watch the couple more closely. And I found that in his evident care and concern for her, that lady's husband truly did show signs of greatness. Love was not blind. But love had drawn forth qualities from this man which the rest of the world had probably never seen, enabling him to sensitively serve the needs of his crippled wife. Love had brought out the best in him, and had cemented their marriage into a union of heartwarming closeness. Love can do that.

WE'RE GETTING OLDER, AND BETTER

Marriage should improve with age, much as a bottle of fine wine becomes more valuable and rare with the passing of time. How wonderful it would be if each of us could look into the eyes of our spouse on the occasion of our golden anniversary and say what a dear Christian man from our church at Hide-A-Way Lake did of his beloved wife: "She is all I'll ever get; she is all I'll ever need; she is all I'll ever want."

As we turn to the final pages of the Song of Solomon, we'll observe another marriage which has improved with age. Wedded life for Solomon and Shulamith just keeps getting better and better. Their first night as husband and wife was one of high passion, yet there was an awkwardness, a formality, to their lovemaking. They were experiencing each other sexually for the first time, and there was a natural tentativeness, an understandable shyness. On their wedding night, Solomon did not speak of Shulamith as sensually as he would be able to do later, as we shall see in chapter 7.

Remember also that Solomon did not praise his wife's more intimate features when she came to him in the garden following their first conflict (see 6:4-10). His words there contained nothing of the erotic. He even begged her to avert her eyes so that he would not be aroused (6:5). The lovers had to deal with the challenge besetting their relationship before the physical could be rightly resumed.

As Song 7 opens, we find our couple alone, once again in

a palace bedroom as on their wedding night. Judging from the freedom with which they relate to each other, there is good reason to believe that the time is years after the wedding. Possibly it is around their fifth, tenth, maybe even twenty-fifth anniversary. While we're not sure when the events occur, it does seem that their marital ship has been plowing though the waters for quite awhile.

I've called this episode from the love diary of our couple "communion" because Solomon and Shulamith are achieving the closeness possible with mature love. They are reaping the fruitful harvest of years together. And you might say that for them reality exceeds their expectations.

IMPROVING WITH TIME—SONG 7:2-11

King to Bride

7:2　How beautiful are your feet in sandals, O
　　　prince's daughter.
　　　The curves of your thighs are like ornaments,
　　　the work of the hands of an artist.

3　Your navel is a rounded goblet never lacking
　　　mixed wine.
　　　Your abdomen is a stack of wheat enclosed with
　　　lilies.

4　Your two breasts are like two fawns, twins of a
　　　gazelle.

5　Your neck is like a tower of ivory.
　　　Your eyes are like the pools in Heshbon
　　　by the gates of the populous city.
　　　Your nose is like a tower in Lebanon keeping
　　　watch over Damascus.

6　Your head crowns you as Carmel.
　　　And the flowing locks of your head are like
　　　purple threads.
　　　The king is held captive by your tresses.

7　How beautiful and how pleasant you are—love
　　　in (your) exquisite delights.

8   This your stature is comparable to a palm tree,
  and your breasts to its clusters.
9   I say, "I will climb the palm tree;
  I will take hold of its fruit stalks;
  Oh, may your breasts be like clusters of the vine
   and the fragrance of your breath like apples
10 and your mouth like the best wine . . . "

Bride (to King)

 . . . going down smoothly for my beloved,
 flowing gently through the lips of the sleeping
  ones.

(in soliloquy)

11 I am my beloved's and his desire is for me.

The night of love which begins Song 7 bears much resemblance to the wedding night seen in chapter 4. In both instances, Solomon initiates the lovemaking by praising his wife. Glickman points out that, while the king had mentioned seven characteristics of his bride's beauty in chapter 4, he describes ten of Shulamith's lovely qualities during this later night of pleasure. In Scripture, the numbers seven and ten are often used to denote perfection or completeness. As the lovers join once again in the Song, Shulamith has, if anything, become more splendid, more "perfect" to her husband than before. His compliments now are tenfold (Glickman 1976, 84-85). Indeed, as the years go by, husband and wife should become closer and more precious to each other—and more appreciative of each other.

There is perhaps another reason why Solomon speaks these additional words of praise to his beloved: there is simply more to talk about! They are more familiar with each other, and with this deeper familiarity has come increased freedom. There is an openness about their relationship. They are no longer sweetly shy, tentative, or formal in their words and embraces. They are able to share more freely, more spontaneously, than was possible during their days of newlywed adjustment. No relationship remains where it was on the wedding night; a marriage either progresses or degenerates. In the case of Solomon and his wife, their affection becomes more rich, more rare, more delicious, with age.

What a Woman You Are!

"How beautiful are your feet in sandals, O prince's daughter. The curves of your thighs are like ornaments, the work of the hands of an artist," Solomon tells his lovely wife when they are alone (7:2). Notice that he calls her a "prince's daughter." It is a significant statement when one recalls Shulamith's early days at the palace. When first surrounded by the sophisticated women of the court, she felt out of place, a rustic maiden in the midst of a veritable assembly of perfumed and painted female piranhas (see 1:5-8). Now her demeanor and bearing are those of the daughter of a prince. She is regal and noble. She is no longer a country girl, but a queen, thanks to Solomon's love and devotion. She more than fits in with the palace crowd; she exceeds them in quality. Her deportment is that of true royalty. What a compliment Solomon gives her, as he once more strives to build the self-image and security of the woman he loves.

The king's speech is intimate as well. As their lovemaking begins, he speaks of the beauty of Shulamith's feet, and then the artistic perfection of her thighs (7:2). His eyes move from the tips of her toes upward to the graceful curve of her hips. He had not mentioned either of these portions of her body on their wedding night. Thus there is progression—increasing freedom, increasing familiarity—in their physical relationship.

Solomon continues his praise. "Your navel is a rounded goblet never lacking mixed wine. Your abdomen is a stack of wheat enclosed with lilies," he tells her (7:3). Evidently he is resting his head upon her belly, caressing her stomach. He speaks of wheat and wine—basic food and drink—perhaps suggesting that she sustains him, that he draws strength from her. Truly, their marriage is nourished by this time of intimacy, and indeed she is a sumptuous banquet to her man.

"Your two breasts are like two fawns, twins of a gazelle," he says next, no doubt while caressing them as one might gently stroke a young deer (7:4). Solomon spoke of his bride's breasts in much the same terms on their wedding night—his words were nearly identical to those here (see 4:5). Oh yes, appropriately recalling the wedding night can be a very good idea!

We might also remember that on their first evening as lovers, Solomon began by praising Shulamith's hair, eyes, and face . . . gradually progressing to the "mountain of myrrh and hill of frankincense" which were her breasts (4:6). With the greater sense of familiarity and freedom evident in chapter 7, he begins by complimenting her more intimate parts, his eyes and caresses moving upward as their passion rises.

"Your neck is like a tower of ivory," Solomon tells his beloved in verse 5. I imagine he is rubbing her neck, helping her to escape the tension of the day. Her neck is smooth and white, a "tower" of strength.

RECOGNIZING THE RED LIGHTS

"Your eyes are like the pools in Heshbon by the gate 'of the populous city," says Solomon next (7:5). His gaze moves upward and he looks directly into her eyes. He finds them refreshing, clear and serene as cool pools of water on the outskirts of a bustling, steamy city. Rather than showing fear or alarm, her eyes reflect the peacefulness she has found in him and the easy contentment they share.

Men, if you want to take a reading on the quality of your relationship with your wife, look into her eyes when the two of you are alone together. Much like the lights on the dashboard of a car which flash red when a fan belt breaks, the oil runs low, or the radiator overheats, your wife's eyes can give you clues about the state of your marriage. If she finds it difficult to return your direct gaze, if she glances downward or away from you or seems uncomfortable, it is as if the red lights have come on. She may well feel misunderstood, unimportant, unloved—a sense of grief and hurt replacing the confidence and joy which should be there. There may be emotional wounds desperately in need of healing.

If you, speaking with quiet love as Solomon does, can peer into the eyes of your lover and find that she meets your gaze with a look of calm trust, then the red lights are off. The relationship is on stable ground. Your woman feels significant to you, secure in your affection, safe in your arms.

MORE THAN SKIN DEEP

With her deep, clear eyes, her smooth, white neck, her soft, elegantly-proportioned body, Shulamith is a vision of loveliness to her husband. But Solomon appreciates much more than her outward appearance. She is attractive within, her beauty extending beneath the skin. On this night of mature love, as on the evening of their wedding, he compliments her character (see 4:4,12).

"Your nose is like a tower in Lebanon keeping watch over Damascus. Your head crowns you as Carmel," the king tells his wife (7:5-6). By describing her nose as "a tower in Lebanon," Solomon isn't suggesting that Shulamith has a large nose. If it were so, Solomon, as a sensitive lover, would do well to ignore that feature of her anatomy. She would probably be self-conscious about being large-nosed anyway, and surely he wouldn't broach the subject at a moment of great intimacy. Rather, by likening Shulamith's nose to a tower, he may be commenting on the stately strength of her character that is seen in her face. She is solid, dependable, enduring, tenacious—much as a watchtower guarding against the enemies of the land would have to be.

By saying that Shulamith's head crowns her "as Carmel" (7:6), Solomon gives his lady what to us is a more obvious compliment. First of all, the fact that her head "crowns" her at all suggests that she is regal of bearing. The word "Carmel" is a reference to Mount Carmel, and Solomon's mention of this landmark would have special meaning for his wife.

Mount Carmel is located in northwestern Israel; Shulamith is well acquainted with it. On its slopes, the prophet Elijah would later meet and defeat the prophets of Baal (1 Kings 18:19-40). From the top of Carmel today, one is treated to a gorgeous view of modern day Haifa, the third largest city in Israel. To the west, the blue expanse of the Mediterranean stretches as far as the eye can see. If you've ever seen Mount Shuksan in the Pacific Northwest or Pike's Peak in Colorado, you'll understand what Mount Carmel is to the people of Israel. It is a magnificent, majestic high point in their land.

By comparing his wife to Carmel, Solomon tells her that she is much like that mountain. She is majestically beautiful, imposing and awe-inspiring in appearance. Simply looking at her takes his breath away, much as a snow-capped purpled mountain in all its grandeur causes us to gaze and sigh in wonder and admiration. Perhaps by his words, the king also suggests that Shulamith's character is like that of a mountain: stately, proud, firm, and strong. She is immovable in her convictions and worthy of the highest respect and regard. She is quite a woman in every way!

A Prisoner of Love

Solomon continues to praise his beloved, speaking, for the third time in his Song, of her luxuriant hair (see also 4:1, 6:5). "And the flowing locks of your head are like purple threads," he tells her. "The king is held captive by your tresses" (7:6). Her hair is lovely and long. Its texture is fine, of threadlike silkiness. Yet her locks are not like any threads, but "purple threads"—rich, finespun strands which, since the color purple is symbolic of royalty, would be used in the garment of a king.

So appealing is Shulamith's hair to Solomon that he describes himself as held captive by her flowing tresses (7:6). We can almost picture him gently stroking her hair, running his hands through it, twisting a strand or two around his fingers, as he allows it to entangle him. He is a willing "prisoner," who loves being bound by her locks.

"How beautiful and how pleasant you are—love in (your) exquisite delights," the king says next (7:7). He finds Shulamith altogether attractive and pleasing. She is beautiful to him within and without. And she offers him "exquisite delights"; evidently he appreciates her sweet and tender response to his caresses.

THE HEIGHT OF ROMANCE

As the intensity of the scene builds, Solomon's language grows eloquently and exquisitely more sensual. "This your stature is comparable to a palm tree, and your breasts to its clusters," he says, possibly while his eyes journey up and down her frame. What a creative way to compliment his beloved! By comparing her body to a palm tree, and her breasts to its clusters of fruit, he takes an image familiar to his wife and uses it to express his admiration. He has done this often in their love relationship—earlier, for example, likening her eyes to doves (1:15, 4:1), her cheeks or temples to pomegranates (4:3, 6:7), her loveliness to the beauty of Jerusalem (6:4).

What does it mean for him to compare her to a palm tree? Think about it. A palm tree is graceful and lithe—a vision of elegance as it sways in the breeze. Its fronds offer shade to the weary traveler; its fruit deliciously sustains. All this Shulamith does for her lover, providing refreshment and nourishment as they drink of their cup of love together. Besides, she too sees in him the stateliness of the palm tree. Remember how she described his locks of raven-black hair to the women of the court as "palm leaves" in chapter 5, verse 11. Apparently the palm tree symbol is recognized by both as a poetic illustration of their admiration for each other. It is part of their language of love.

Through his tender words and caresses, Solomon has

prepared Shulamith for the moment of consummation. As
on their wedding night, their lovemaking has been superb-
ly slow. Yet unlike the wedding night, the king does not ask
that his bride bring her thoughts completely to him. Neither does he tell her to put aside her fears (see 4:8). He
doesn't have to; she naturally gives him her full and confident attention as they enjoy each other with reckless—and
familiar—abandon.

Neither does Solomon, as he did on the wedding night,
wait for an invitation from his wife before he proceeds (see
4:16). The lovers are freer with each other now; they have
been together long enough to recognize the "signals." Solomon knows that Shulamith is aroused, ready for the full
expression of their love, and so he makes an announcement: "I say, 'I will climb the palm tree; I will take hold of
its fruit stalks; Oh, may your breasts be like clusters of the
vine and the fragrance of your breath like apples and your
mouth like the best wine . . ." (7:9-10).

She finishes the final sentence for him, ". . . going down
smoothly for my beloved, flowing gently through the lips
of the sleeping ones" (7:10). These evocative words tastefully reveal that consummation has occurred. It is obvious
that Solomon and his wife are one, in spirit and in flesh.

It is amazing how close this pair is, how much they
think alike, how comfortable they have become with each
other. In his announcement, Solomon asks that Shulamith's
breasts be "like clusters of the vine," ripe and full fruit. He
compares the fragrance of her breath to the scent of apples,
and then he likens her mouth—perhaps meaning her kisses—to the finest of wines (7:9-10). Her kisses should be as
smooth wine, adds Shulamith, completing his thoughts.
They should be wine which flows "gently through the lips
of the sleeping ones" (7:10). In other words, the kisses they
exchange as they rest in each other's arms following consummation will be soothing and pleasant, lingering upon
their lips as they fall sweetly asleep. And so, I imagine,
they soon do.

It is interesting that Solomon and Shulamith would
agree that the kisses concluding their lovemaking must be

like "the best wine" (7:9). That choice of words is reminiscent of those spoken by the Lord at the end of the wedding night, when He encouraged the bride and groom, "Eat O loved ones; Drink and be drunk, O lovers" (5:1). Husbands and wives should find their love for each other—and the physical expression of that love—intoxicating.

God had designed us to find sex with our spouse exhilarating. He encourages husbands and wives to enjoy each other enthusiastically. He sanctions the excitement, so much so that if married lovers were caught embracing at the rapture of the church, when Christ will come for His own, they should not be embarrassed. The fact that Solomon and Shulamith relish their physical relationship does not destroy the sacredness of sex in their marriage. They are merely obeying orders—God's orders! The sexual expession of their love nourishes their marriage.

Afterward, they fall peacefully asleep. But before she drifts off, Shulamith says to herself, "I am my beloved's and his desire is for me" (7:11). It is a slightly-altered version of the phrase she has uttered twice before (see 2:16, 6:3). She is pleased to be Solomon's cherished possession, his desirable treasure. We have seen how his love has increased her self-esteem and made her secure. She feels she fully belongs to him and that he finds her completely captivating. As the lyrics to a song popular a few years ago aptly put it: "After the lovin', I'm still in love with you." Indeed, Solomon and Shulamith are perhaps now even more in love with each other, the intensity of their affection increased by a night at the height of romance.

A SECOND HONEYMOON—SONG 7:12–8:3

> *Bride to King*
> 7:12 Come, my beloved, let us go out into the country.
> Let us spend the night in the villages.
> 13 Let us rise early to the vineyards.
> Let us see whether the vine has budded
> and its blossoms have opened
> and whether the pomegranates have bloomed.
> There I will give my caresses to you.

14 The mandrakes have given forth fragrance
   and over our doors are all choice fruits—
   both new and old, which I have stored up for
   you, my beloved.

8:1 Oh that you were like a brother to me
   who nursed at the breasts of my mother.
   If I found you outdoors I would kiss you,
   and no one would despise me either.

2 I would lead you;
   I would bring you to the house of my mother.
   You would instruct me.
   I would give you spiced wine to drink, the nectar
   of my pomegranate.

3 Oh may his left hand be under my head and his
   right hand embrace me.

to Daughters of Jerusalem

4 I adjure you, O daughters of Jerusalem,
   not to arouse, not to awaken love until it
   pleases.

From the evening of pleasurable passion we've witnessed, the setting of the Song changes to that of a day in the spring. Perhaps it is the next morning—maybe it is much later—as verse 11 begins.

The last time that springtime was mentioned in the Song was in chapter 2, when Solomon journeyed to Lebanon, apparently with the intention of proposing to Shulamith. The flowers were bursting forth, the birds were singing in the trees, and he was heading north with the engagement ring in the pocket of his robe (see 2:1-17).

Now it is spring again and the traditional season of romance calls for a second honeymoon. Shulamith longs to visit the place where their love began, so they embark on a return trip to Lebanon.

"Come my beloved, let us go out into the country," Shulamith urges her lover. "Let us spend the night in the villages. Let us rise early in the vineyards" (7:12-13). She asks him to come away with her, to temporarily forget the demands of the kingdom and go on a little vacation. The remark about their rising "early in the vineyards" tells him that it is to Lebanon that she desires to go. It was, after all, in the vineyards leased by her family where Solomon first spied his lovely country girl.

They will be traveling to Lebanon so that they might, as Shulamith puts it, "see whether the vine has budded and its blossoms have opened and whether the pomegranates have bloomed" (7:13). They'll be looking for signs that spring has arrived. But they will also be seeking refreshment and renewal in their love relationship.

In Segal's *The Tenth Measure,* mentioned earlier, the character Alexandra longs for her husband, Eleazar Ben Yair, to accompany her from the hills of Masada to the springs of En-Gedi. Why? It is because at En-Gedi their love first blossomed; it is their special place.

Like Alexandra, Shulamith simply wants to revisit the site where the love she shares with Solomon began. "There," she promises the king, "I will give my caresses to you" (7:13). For the first time in the Song, we see Shulamith initiating the physical. Familiarity spawns freedom—and she voices her intentions without reservation. I imagine Solomon orders his servants to pack the bags right away! How exciting that Shulamith can speak of sexual intimacy without feeling awkward or ashamed!

In fact, she has prepared a basketful of "goodies" for Solomon. "The mandrakes have given forth fragrance and over our doors are all choice fruits," Shulamith tells the king, "both new and old, which I have stored up for you, my beloved" (7:14). Mandrakes were believed by the ancients to have aphrodisiac qualities, so you can imagine that the "treats" Shulamith has in store for her husband will be delectable indeed. She tastefully, yet most directly, requests that they make love, and the liberty she feels to do so is evidence that their relationship is growing deeper, stronger, more secure.

Shulamith's reference to mandrakes calls to mind Rachel's request for such fruit in Genesis 30:14. Rachel's desire for mandrakes was prompted by her deep longing to have a child. Perhaps children are also on Shulamith's mind; only a few verses later, she will make mention of a woman in labor (see 8:5). Yet it is interesting that never in the Song do the lovers speak of procreation as the reason for their physical relationship. In fact, Scripture contains no record that Solomon and Shulamith ever had children together. God approved of their sexual intimacy in and of itself.

LET'S PRETEND

As she continues to freely speak what is on her mind and heart, Shulamith becomes rather playful. Teasingly, she says to Solomon, "Oh that you were a brother to me who nursed at the breasts of my mother. If I found you outdoors I would kiss you, and no one would despise me either" (8:1). While their culture frowned upon public demonstrations of affection between husbands and wives, it was acceptable for brothers and sisters or other family members to embrace in front of others. Shulamith wishes she could give Solomon hugs and kisses so that all the world might see! Of course, she cannot do this because he is her husband, and such behavior in public would be regarded contemptuously. But if he were her brother, that would be different. So Shulamith playfully pretends that she'd like it to be so.

Still whimsically imagining that she wants Solomon as her brother, she goes on to say, "I would lead you; I would bring you to the house of my mother. You would instruct me" (8:2). Her words must be charming to the king; probably he laughs in delight at her lighthearted playacting. If he were her brother, she would lead him to her mother's house. Yet once there, she would desire him to instruct her; she would want him to assume the leadership.

The tone of Shulamith's speech becomes more somewhat serious and a great deal more sensual. Still speaking of their imaginary trip to the house of her mother, she makes Solomon a promise, "I would give you spiced wine to drink, the nectar of my pomegranate" (8:2). Remember that in the past she has referred to his kisses as wine (see 1:2, 7:10). He has described the rosiness of her cheeks as the color of the pomegranate (see 4:3, 6:7). Perhaps by offering the spiced wine of her pomegranate to her "brother," Shulamith is gleefully telling Solomon that she'd like to shower him with kisses; they would proceed from her mouth, which she may be referring to as a rosy-red "pomegranate."

Certainly she is interested in receiving more than brotherly attention from her man! "Oh may his left hand be under my head and his right hand embrace me," she longingly sighs in verse 3. The pretense is over, the mirthful musing gives way to an expression of genuine desire.

Isn't it special that Shulamith feels so comfortable with Solomon that she can spin such playful yarns? She knows he will not laugh at her, but with her. I believe that the wishes she voices in the process of pretending are shared by many wives, too. Let me explain.

Notice that Shulamith first utters a desire that her husband be as a brother to her. As such, they would be playmates. In public they'd have fun together—they'd play! I believe that most wives wish their husband would be their companion in leisure, at least some of the time. Going to the movies, picnicking in the park, hiking a mountain trail, even walking around the neighborhood—these are all ways in which modern couples can "play" together.

Second, in the privacy of her mother's house, Shulamith requests that Solomon "instruct" her. She wants him to open his heart, share his thoughts and knowledge and understanding of life with her. She wants him to communicate in private. I've never met a woman yet who doesn't want this from her man.

And finally, Shulamith longs for Solomon to be her lover. God intends that each woman desire her husband sexually. Playful brother, communicative friend, caring lover—these are the roles wives wish their husbands would play . . . and play for keeps!

REAPING THE 'REWARDS

Shulamith closes this section of her reflections with a final warning to the women of the court: "I adjure you, O daughters of Jerusalem, not to arouse, not to awaken love until it pleases" (8:4). She has given this advice twice previously, first making the statement when she felt the stirrings of sexual yearning during their courtship (2:7). The physical part of their relationship could not be rushed; it had to wait for their marriage.

Shortly before their wedding, Shulamith made the remark again (3:5). As she anticipated the glamour of the royal procession and the exhilirating newness of the wedding night, she was glad that Solomon and she had exercised self-control till then. She highly recommended restraint until the time was right. She soon was to know the joy of sexual love, properly expressed (see 4:1–5:1).

And now, because she and Solomon have not forced their love but have allowed it to develop and grow of its own accord, she feels free to speak of sexual desires and to initiate the physical. Through the years they have worked on their total relationship: resolving conflicts, developing better communication, striving for increased sensitivity. Now they are reaping the fruit of time well spent, reveling in the rewards of mature love.

WHAT IS THIS THING CALLED LOVE?—SONG 8:5-14

> *Poet*
> 8:5 Who is this coming from the wilderness, leaning
>   on her beloved?
> *Bride to King*
>   Beneath the apple tree I awakened you;
>   there your mother was in labor with you;
>   there she was in labor and gave you birth.
>   6 Put me as a seal upon your heart,
>   As a seal upon your arm.
>   For strong as death is love.
>   Relentless as Sheol is jealousy.
>   Its flashes are flashes of fire,
>   the flame of Yahweh.
>   7 Many waters cannot extinguish this love
>   and many rivers will not drown it.

If a man were to give all the possessions of his
house for love, he would be utterly despised.

Brothers of the Bride

8 We have a little sister and she has no breasts.
What shall we do for our sister for the day on
which she is spoken for?

9 If she is a wall,
we shall build on her a battlement of silver,
But if she is a door,
we shall enclose her with planks of cedar.

Bride (to all)

10 I was a wall and my breasts were like towers.
Then I became in his eyes as one who finds
peace.

11 A vineyard belonged to Solomon at Baal Hamon.
He gave the vineyard to caretakers; each one was
to bring a thousand shekels of silver for its
fruit.

12 My own vineyard belongs to me.

to King

The thousand are for you, O Solomon,
and two hundred for the caretakers of the
fruit.

King to Bride

13 O you who dwell in the gardens,
(My) companions are listening for your voice.
Let me hear it.

Bride to King

14 Hurry, my beloved,
And be like a gazelle or a young stag
on the mountains of spices.

As Solomon's Song draws to a close, the king and his
beloved wife take the vacation to Lebanon which she has
requested. "Who is this coming from the wilderness, lean-
ing on her beloved?" asks the poet or narrator in verse 5.
Who indeed? It is Shulamith accompanying her husband
as they return to the place where their love first bloomed.
The last portion of the Song is more than a record of this

second honeymoon, however. As we shall see, the inspiring Holy Spirit leaves us with reflections on the nature of love as we come to the end of Solomon's greatest lyric.

MADE FOR EACH OTHER

Shulamith speaks to her lover in verse 5: "Beneath the apple tree I awakened you; there your mother was in labor with you; there she was in labor and gave you birth." Remember that before leaving Jerusalem, she had cautioned the palace ladies not to awaken love until the proper moment. There she referred primarily to sexual love. But there is another sense in which love must not be roused prematurely: love must wait for the right lover to come along!

Solomon is the man for Shulamith; they are well-suited to each other, and their love awakens as they realize they are meant to be together. Too many times young people— pressured because their friends have made the trip down the aisle, perhaps worried that they'll be "doomed" to life alone—are not willing to wait for the right man or woman to come along. So they latch on to the most convenient partner available and proceed with the program.

Such couples want to get married for the sake of getting married. They're really more enchanted with the idea of the wedding than with the one they plan to wed. And after' the altar may well come the disaster of divorce.

"We married too young." "We had nothing in common." I don't know what I saw in him in the first place." Bitter comments such as these have often fallen from the lips of the frustrated wives and husbands who sit in my office and hope that their marriage can be patched up . . . or dissolved.

I guess Patti Roberts puts it as well as anyone who has lived through the shattering trauma of divorce. When writing of the early days of her engagement to Richard, she recalls, "We were two kids in love with the idea of being in love and sincerely trying to be in love with each other" (Roberts 1983, 57). They were enamored of the propects of playing house, but in the grown-up world of married life the players have got to be ready. When Shulamith finds him under the "apple tree," a figurative expression for their love, Solomon is prepared. The time is right for love. They are made for each other.

THE SACRIFICE—NO PAIN, NO GAIN

As she reflects upon the birth of their love, Shulamith also makes mention of Solomon's physical birth (8:5). In some ways the two are very similar. Both require sacrifice and both involve pain. The pain felt by a woman in childbirth is sharp and piercing. Comedienne Carol Burnett once suggested that labor pain could be simulated by grasping your lower lip and pulling it up over your head! Any mother who has borne a child will tell you that the process involves sacrifice. Shulamith and Solomon too have experienced their share of pain and sacrifice as their love has grown.

Shulamith knew the agony of insecurity as the women of the court taunted her in chapter 1. Her love for Solomon propelled her to the palace, thrusting her into an environment in which she felt at best uncomfortable. It was a sacrifice she willingly made. Later she knew the pain of separation from her lover as he left her in Lebanon to await their wedding day. Fearful dreams tortured her sleep (3:1-5). Yet the ecstasy of the wedding night more than made up for the sacrifice of separation.

Solomon likewise dealt with his share of pain. His return to Jerusalem after proposing to Shulamith must have been a lonely time for him. Later he would meet the hurtful sting of Shulamith's indifference. He answered this challenge to their relationship with sacrificial love and sensitivity (5:2–6:10).

Almost any woman who has labored to give birth to a child will tell you that the process involves sacrifice but that it is worth it. Most will claim to have forgotten the birth pangs by the time their newborn baby rests in their arms. For Solomon and Shulamith the sacrifice has been worthwhile as well; the love that is born partly of the pain they have known is something precious and special.

SEALED WITH A STRENGTH THAT ENDURES

Shulamith continues her reflections on love by making this request of her man, "Put me as a seal upon your heart, As a seal upon your arm" (8:6). Her desire is to be Solomon's permanent possession, his eternal lover. She wants to be assured of his affection, sealed in him forever. And it is God's plan that their love would endure.

Why? As Shulamith says next, "For strong as death is love. Relentless as Sheol is jealousy. Its flashes are flashes of fire, the flame of Yahweh" (8:6). Love possesses with a supernatural strength. It seals two lovers together even as the grave seals its dead. It is jealous, but with the healthy jealousy of rightful ownership: two who truly love each other also truly belong to each other. Love's jealous flashes of fire come from Yahweh, the Lord Himself, for He is the giver of love.

Love is designed by God to be strong. In Shulamith's words, "Many waters cannot extinguish this love and rivers will not drown it" (8:7). She is saying that their love will never be quenched; it will never surrender; it will never desert; it will never depart. It is the essence of commitment, as they have pledged themselves to each other and saved themselves for each other.

SACRED—BEYOND PRICE

Shulamith concludes her meditations on the nature of love as she speaks of its inestimable value: "If a man were to give all the possessions of his house for love, he would be utterly despised" (8:7). Why would a man who sold everything for love be rejected? It is because love is not for sale. No adequate price tag can ever be attached to it.

Trying to set a value upon love is to cheapen it, for it is more rare than the most exquisite treasure imaginable. And once found, love must handled with care—with the same precision, gentleness, and painstaking patience that a jeweler must use when cutting a diamond. We have seen Solomon and Shulamith do just that, and their marriage has thrived.

SAVED FOR EACH OTHER

One reason that Solomon and Shulamith are able to experience the full joy of their love is that they have been saved for each other. Shulamith's brothers are the ones she must thank for that. And she is grateful to her family, as we shall observe. Perhaps it wasn't always so. Remember that when she defended herself to the women of the palace, she exclaimed that her brothers had forced her to work in the vineyards and thus she had had no time to care for her own appearance, her own "vineyard" (1:5-6). While growing up, she may have resented her brothers for their supposed cruelty. Yet as the brothers begin to speak in the Song, we see that their motives are far from mean.

"We have a little sister and she has no breasts," Shulamith's brothers explain (8:8). Perhaps they are speaking aloud; possibly Shulamith is merely recalling words she heard as a child. Whatever the case, the brothers were faced with a problem when Shulamith was a little girl. Evidently her father was dead, and she became their responsibility. How could they keep her pure and chaste until the day of her wedding? As the brothers put it, "What shall we do for our sister for the day on which she is spoken for?" (8:8). It is a perplexing question, and this is their solution.

"If she is a wall," reveal the brothers, "we shall build on her a battlement of silver, But if she is a door, we shall enclose her with planks of cedar" (8:9). If Shulamith stands firm against the advances of men, she will be as a "wall," unyielding and chaste. If so, they will honor her, adorning her with "a battlement of silver." But if she is promiscuous, an open "door" to the advances of men, they will punish her. The image of her being enclosed "with planks of cedar" suggests that she would be penned up, kept confined, placed on restriction, as my teenagers used to say.

Many young ladies would have rebelled against this show of "brotherly love," considering it too stringent and even downright cruel. But Shulamith cooperates with the wishes of her family. And she is glad that she did! "I was a wall," she states firmly, "and my breasts were towers" (8:10).

Why is she pleased that she saved herself so? The answer is given in verse 10, where Shulamith says, "Then I became in his eyes as one who finds peace." It is as if she is saying, "I'm so glad I waited so that I could give myself fully to you, my husband!" She finds peace in the arms of her lover, and one reason is that she does not come to the marriage plagued by the guilt of past indiscretions. There is nothing in her history to mar her enjoyment of her relationship with Solomon. Saying no is well worth the effort!

Over and over again Scripture teaches that we only give away our virginity once. In Genesis 39, the wife of Potiphar attempts to entice Joseph to do just that, and he refuses, instead fleeing the situation (see 39:6-12). God ultimately honors Joseph tremendously because of his response, too. A few chapters later in Genesis we read that he has been given a worthy wife and is the father of two precious sons (41:50-52).

The Lord likes us to follow His time schedule in our life. Shulamith is wonderfully happy that she observed God's schedule and kept herself for Solomon. In fact, she uses a pun in the Hebrew to describe her joy. As Glickman suggests, another translation of verse 10 could read, "Shulamith found her Shalom (peace) in Shulamoh (Solomon)" (Glickman 1976, 108).

ONE ENCHANTED EVENING

Of course it must have been lonely for her waiting in that vineyard all those years! Beginning in verse 11, Shulamith recalls the magic moment when she meets the man of her dreams. Evidently she is speaking before several others, possibly her family and friends.

"A vineyard belonged to Solomon at Baal Hamon," she reminds all who will listen (8:11). "He gave the vineyard to caretakers; each one was to bring a thousand shekels of silver for its fruit" (8:11). This is the vineyard which has been leased to Shulamith's family; it is the place where she has been forced by her brothers to work. She probably assumes that she will never meet an eligible man while slaving with those grapes! And then he comes! Isn't it terrific how God rewards obedience in the most unexpected ways?

Shulamith's brothers are to bring to Solomon "a thousand shekels of silver" in payment for the use of his land. Yet Shulamith reminds her lover that her own vineyard—her whole being—belongs to her (8:12). "The thousand are for you, O Solomon, and two hundred for the caretakers of the fruit," she exclaims (8:12). She freely gives herself to him—physically, emotionally, intellectually, spiritually.

Yet she also reminds him of the debt of gratitude they both owe to her family, "the caretakers of the fruit," who raised her well and helped prepare her for him. Since they are visiting her relatives in Lebanon at the time, perhaps Solomon takes the opportunity to thank his in-laws for their part in readying his bride for him. Expressing such appreciation to your spouse's family is never a bad idea!

Precious to Each Other

Solomon next turns to Shulamith and requests of her, "O you who dwell in the gardens, (My) companions are listening for your voice. Let me hear it" (8:13). He tactfully asks for her undivided attention. She has been speaking with family and friends—the companions who listen for her voice—but now he wants to be alone with her.

By reminding Shulamith that she is the one who dwells "in the gardens," Solomon hearkens back to their wedding night. Then he had spoken of her as "a garden locked . . . a spring locked, a fountain sealed" (4:12). And following their lovemaking he had announced, "I have come into my garden, my sister, my bride" (5:1). By mentioning the idea of the garden in chapter 8, verse 13, he delicately suggests that they leave the assembled company so that they might enjoy each other sexually.

Apparently they do adjourn to a place of privacy, because the next words in the Song are those of Shulamith, who says to the king, "Hurry, my beloved, And be a gazelle or a young stag on the mountains of spices" (8:14). With this final expression of physical desire, Solomon's Song closes. Their "second honeymoon" has indeed led to a new season of love for them. The fire in their relationship had never been extinguished—but by visiting the site of its original sparks, they have fanned the flames of romance.

Notice also that Shulamith asks Solomon to "be a gazelle" upon her "mountains of spices." Before their wedding she had referred to her breasts simply as the "mountains of separation" (2:17). Now she thinks of them, and of herself, as more rich, more rare, more exquisite. Solomon's love has done this for her; their years together have caused her to see herself as he sees her.

What a lovely note on which to end this incredibly romantic ballad! As Solomon's Song has unfolded, we've seen the courtship of the lovers and witnessed their commitment. We've watched as they have handled a challenge to their love. Now we observe the sweetness of communion, the beauty of two who have become one in every sense of the word. That is what marriage should be all about.

LESSONS

Here are some final lessons from the wisdom of Solomon and Shulamith—and of course from the Holy Spirit.

Lesson one: men, *no matter what, strive to build up the self-image of your wife.* What she is in your eyes is more important to her than just about anything else in the world. If you don't take time to honestly praise her, you'll be dealing her ego a severe blow. Throughout the Song, we see Solomon lavishing Shulamith with genuine compliments.

Lesson two: this one also goes to the men. *Always minister to your wife's need for security.* Emphasize the fact that you'll be there for her. Let her know that you are committed to your marriage and you'll never give up, back out, run off, or even mention the dirty word *divorce*. Solomon never so much as hints to Shulamith that he regrets marrying her. He consistently assures her of his commitment to her and to their relationship.

Lesson three: *with mature love comes a greater sense of freedom and familiarity.* As their marriage progresses, Shulamith feels increasingly free to share her desires with Solomon. No doubt this is because he has worked through the years to meet her self-image and security needs.

Four: *it can be good for the vitality of a marriage to relive meaningful experiences of the past.* Solomon and Shulamith find new romance as they journey to the place where their love began. Second honeymoons can refresh and renew a relationship.

On our twenty-fifth anniversary, Pearl and I found ourselves in Salem, Oregon, where we had been married. I was speaking at a conference there, but we managed to slip away and pay a visit to the church where we were wed. We walked the sanctuary together. Upon exiting the church, we drove to where our getaway car had been hidden on the night of our wedding. With me behind the wheel and Pearl at my side, we retraced the escape route we had taken so long ago. What a fun-filled, memorable evening it was!

Lesson five: *we can only give away our virginity once.* It's best to be a "wall," as Shulamith was, than a "door," open to the advances of others. What if it's too late for you? Is there any hope? Yes! Come to the Lord today. Ask His forgiveness for past indiscretions. 1 John 1:9 assures us: "If we confess our sins, He is faithful and righteous to forgive us our sins and to cleanse us from all unrighteousness" (NASB). Experience the freedom of His pardon and allow His

Spirit to work in your life to enable you to turn away from disobedience.

No sin is too great for Him to conquer. And, no matter what you have done, He will be able to use you effectively if you are open to His guidance and are willing to follow. If you think your past is too scarlet, just remember that Rahab the harlot, who sheltered the Israelite spies in Joshua 2, was given the privilege of becoming the mother of Boaz. She is included in the genealogy of Jesus Christ (see Matthew 1:5)! These words of the Lord in Isaiah 1:18 should be of encouragement:

> "Come now, and let us reason together,"
> Says the LORD,
> "Though your sins are as scarlet,
> They will be white as snow;
> Though they are red like crimson,
> They will be like wool" (NASB).

Lesson six: *God approves of the sexual relationship between a husband and a wife in and of itself.* He desires us to delight in each other. If children are born to a union, they are a gift from Him. But even if a couple has no children, He still sanctions the physical. In 1 Samuel 1:7, Hannah weeps because of her barrenness. Her husband Elkanah approaches her with these words of comfort, "Hannah, why do you weep and why do you not eat and why is your heart sad? Am I not better to you than ten sons?" (1 Samuel 1:9 NASB). Sons or no sons, he still loves her. Children are a blessing, yes, but a childless marriage should still be one of commitment and closeness.

Lesson seven: *the best lover is the best servant.* Throughout the Song, Solomon concerns himself with the welfare of his woman. He is the epitome of a sensitive, successful leader in their marriage because he is such an unselfish servant. The happiness which Shulamith and he share is proof positive that he is doing things the right way.

The love which Solomon faithfully demonstrates to his

wife is the agape love of which we've spoken earlier. It's the sacrificial love which sent Jesus Christ to Calvary . . . and which can empower husbands and wives to unselfishly serve the needs of their mate. It is a gift of the Spirit of God working in the life of a believer who has accepted Christ as Savior and Lord. You can be a channel of agape love to your spouse. It's a matter of spending time with God in fellowship, study, and prayer; it's a result of earnestly asking Him to make you sensitive to the needs of your partner; and it is the outcome of total Christ-centered commitment to your marriage.

You're not there yet? Don't worry, God is not through with you yet! As Paul states in Philippians 1:6, "For I am confident of this very thing, that He who began a good work in you will perfect it until the day of Christ Jesus" (NASB).

His Love for Us

As we have seen in the final chapters of the Song of Solomon, genuine love involves sacrifice; it seals with an enduring strength; it is sacred beyond measure. So should be the love of a man and a woman. And beyond question, so is the love of God for us.

His love sacrifices. Christ's death on the cross is the ultimate example of His sacrificial love for us. He endured the agony of an excruciating and humiliating execution so that His children might live eternally with Him.

As Christians we are called to experience our share of pain and sacrifice. There is the pain of separation from our Lord. There are the trials which He permits in our life so we will grow more like Him. Our sacrifice lasts but a fleeting moment in the span of eternity, however. Soon we shall be with Him and He will wipe away all our tears (see Revelation 21:4).

His love seals with unyielding strength. Ephesians 4:30 says, "Do not grieve the Holy Spirit of God, by whom you were sealed for the day of redemption" (NASB). When we receive Christ as Savior, God's Spirit seals us eternally;

we've made an everlasting transaction. His seal represents His ownership of us and our security in Him.

During my seminary days in Dallas, I worked at a freight line company, loading trucks. Once each truck was fully loaded, the door was shut and a metal seal was clipped around the latch. The door could no longer be opened without breaking the seal; it was a sign that the goods inside were safe. Anyone breaking the seal before the truck reached its destination would be guilty of a felony and a federal offense. In much the same way does God seal us with His Spirit at our moment of salvation. While a criminal might steal from a sealed truck, nothing can break the Lord's seal upon His own. In the words of the apostle Paul in Romans 8:38-39:

> For I am convinced that neither death, nor life, nor angels, nor principalities, nor things present, nor things to come, nor powers, nor height, nor depth, nor any other created thing, shall be able to separate us from the love of God which is in Christ Jesus our Lord" (NASB, see also John 10:28-29).

His love is sacred, beyond price. God's love cannot be bought, sold, or earned by human means. It can only be received as we accept Christ. The riches He offers His children are unimaginably grand as well. When we get to heaven we'll exclaim, much as the wedding guests at Cana of Galilee did, "You've saved the best till now!" (see John 2:10). As Paul writes, "Eye hath not seen, nor ear heard, neither have entered into the heart of man, the things which God hath prepared for them that love him" (1 Corinthians 2:9 KJV). What a way to go!

IN THE MEANTIME

What are we supposed to do while we wait for our heavenly reward? The answer is easy. While we wait, we serve. Selfishness dictates, yet love wants to serve. We start with the Lord, our wife, our husband, our sons and daughters, and others—and we start today. Grab your towel and start washing feet! Time is wasting . . . and you will want to hear, "Well done, thou good and faithful servant," when it's all over.

Questions for Personal or Group Study

1. As Solomon and Shulamith join once more as lovers in chapter 7 of the Song, what are some of the creative ways in which the king praises his wife (see 7:1-10)?

2. What do Shulamith's words in Song 7:11 reveal about her perceptions of the security of her marriage?

3. Why does Shulamith desire to go on a "second honeymoon" with her husband (see 7:12-13)? How does the promise she makes Solomon in chapter 7, verse 13, reveal that she feels freedom and familiarity in their relationship?

4. How do verses 1-3 of chapter 8 illustrate that Shulamith desires Solomon to be her brother, friend, and lover?

5. What did Shulamith's brothers decide to do while she was growing up to prepare her for marriage (see 8:8-9)? Is she grateful to them for their efforts (see 8:10-12)? Explain.

8

Going for the Gold

Even to your old age and gray hairs I am he, I am he who will sustain you" (Isaiah 46:4 NIV).

LOOK FOR LOVE?

Author Mark Baker interviewed some 150 Vietnam veterans while gathering material for his book, *NAM*. In that work, Baker recounts a host of heart-wrenching, frequently pathetic, often sordid and sickening stories of the war. One such account follows—the tale of a young man's stupid and senseless mistake on what should have been his last night in relative safety. This young serviceman was scheduled to report for duty on the front lines the following day; he never made it. As Baker, recording another soldier's version of the incident, writes:

> This eighteen-year-old kid was celebrating one night, because the next morning was going to be his first time through there. He was going to do it up big, get drunk and get himself a prostitute and spend the night doing whatever it is they do.
>
> She was a sweet little thing. She brought a satchel charge into his APC [armored personnel carrier] with her. They did their thing. She went home, and shortly thereafter the charge blew up. Of course, being in a confined area, he not only got the shrapnel, he got the full load. He came in with no arms and his legs were

gone below the knee. All he had was a head and a trunk.

I was the lucky one. I got to take care of him. He was so bad, he got a "special": one nurse just for him.

He had these huge gaping holes and he had lost so much blood. You give somebody a lot of blood and they have problems coagulating. They couldn't stop this kid from bleeding. So he's got these big dressings on his stumps that are bleeding and his arms are bleeding. He's recovering from the anesthesia. Yet, you don't want him to recover, because he's going to freak out when he sees what's left of him.

Plus, there were some other guys on the ward who knew him and they are waking up. They see him and they're going nuts. There's nothing you can do for them. All you can say is, "If you don't like it, man, you can just look the other way. I'm sorry, but there's just nothing that we can do about it."

Every time the kid tried to open his eyes or even lift his head to see how he was, we just gave him a blast of morphine. It took him two days to die. What an awful price to pay for a one-night stand (Baker 1983, 216-217).

That young soldier did pay an awesome price for an evening's "pleasure." This very night, many married men will follow in his footsteps, searching for extramarital sex. Their limbs may not be blown apart, but it's possible that marriages eventually will be. Too many marital boats end up crashing against the rocky shoals of the sea of matrimony because of one-night stands, sporadic unfaithfulness, or long-standing affairs.

Searching for love in all the wrong places is dangerous. It is contrary to God's plan, as well, for He has designed marriage as the human arena for sexual, intellectual, emotional, and spiritual fulfillment (see 1 Thessalonians 4:3-8).

King David—no stranger to sexual disobedience—describes the consequences of immorality in Psalm 32:3-4, where he writes about the aftereffects of his affair with

Bathsheba and his subsequent murder of her husband,
Uriah the Hittite. David's unconfessed sin resulted in a
period of devastating, lingering guilt during which he frequently felt the chastening hand of the Lord. In the king's
words:

> When I kept silent,
>   my bones wasted away
>   through my groaning all day long
> For day and night
>   your hand was heavy upon me,
> my strength was sapped
>   as in the heat of the summer (NIV).

Illicit sex brings with it its own measure of ugliness.
Temporarily pleasurable, it leaves in its wake the spreading
stain of guilt, the nagging fear of exposure, the ominous
promise that others will be hurt as they learn of the indiscretion. In the Lord's scheme of things, the love affairs we
have should ever and always be with the one we married!

RUNNING THE RACE

Having a love affair with one's own wife or husband
takes time . . . and should encompass a lifetime. In the
language of running, marriage is not a fast sprint, started
by a shotgun and ended in a spurt. Its participants
shouldn't plan on crossing the finish line until decades
after the race begins. No disqualifications should be permitted enroute, no dropouts allowed. Just about the only
legitimate, scriptural way out of the event is to die in mid-
race—which really only means that the finish line has
been reached a little sooner than expected.

No, marriage is not a fast sprint. Instead, I believe that it
is more like a marathon. And notice that I've referred to
husbands and wives as "participants" in the race of matrimony, not "contestants." There is a world of difference
because most of the runners involved in marathons are not
concerned with competition; they simply are trying to finish, and hopefully to finish well.

If you have ever raced in a real marathon, you know that much of the running is tough. It is uphill and into the wind. Much of married life is like that as well—difficult, yet so worth the effort. I am reminded of running with my friend Doug one time as we trained together for a marathon. We were getting close to the end of that day's fifteen miles; the going was getting tough and I was becoming more weary with each step. Slowly and painfully we jogged uphill. Doug, looking ahead, made a remark I will always remember: "After we climb this one, the rest of the way is a piece of cake."

You might say that after a husband and wife reach the top of the hill in their marriage, the rest of the way is a sweet piece of cake, too. What is that hilltop summit? I figure it's the fifty year mark—the golden anniversary (or thereabouts). Yet far more runners will finish marathons of 26.2 miles than will complete marriages of fifty or more years. Perhaps we ought to do something about that. I have an idea.

LET'S DO STAND ON CEREMONY

Reaching fifty years of marriage is a noteworthy, newsworthy achievement. Why don't we, as a society, treat it as such? We give distinguished medals of honor, purple hearts, stars, ribbons, and stripes to our battlefield heroes. Our Olympic athletes compete for the gold, the silver, and the bronze. Yet all our couples who make it to the fifty-year mark get is a picture in the paper and a letter from the President. I'd like to see us do more; in fact, let's launch an all-out campaign to encourage husbands and wives to go for the gold!

We can begin with the printed and spoken word. I've read hundreds of sports stories telling of athletes who overcame tremendous handicaps to achieve glorious successes. I've heard countless war stories outlining the courageous acts of soldiers in combat. But where are the stories of the husbands and wives who manage to clear the hurdles and survive the fires and trials of a half-century of life together? Sometimes these accounts of everyday heroism are lost in the shuffle because we love to read and hear of the sensational, instead. We shouldn't forget that tales of marital triumphs are worth our attention too.

One such story which I recently heard touched me deeply because it involved some very dear friends of ours. Mike and Myrna Schoenfeld have been on the board of our Ministries since its inception. For quite some time now Myrna's mom has suffered from cancer, an excruciatingly painful form of the disease. During much of this last year her condition has been listed as terminal. She has faced crisis after crisis, many times clinging to life by the barest of threads. Repeatedly, the doctors have been amazed at her refusal to surrender when it would have been so much easier for her to let go of life.

We too were astonished at this lady's tremendous will to live, until we learned the reason why. Myrna's parents were scheduled to celebrate their fiftieth wedding anniversary this September and her mother wanted to be around for the occasion! The beautiful end of the story is that she made it; she was able to grasp the gold with her man.

What a treasure a life filled with the memories of fifty years must be! The couples who make it to fifty-plus are worthy of our sincere honor. And those who commit themselves to going for the gold should be encouraged as they run the race together.

FINISHING WELL

My dad, never one to wax sentimental at such events as anniversaries, made an insightful remark to me on the occasion of his fiftieth. When asked how he and Mom had made it that far, he looked at me and, with a twinkle in his eye and a grin on his face, said, "In our day, we didn't have an option. When we had problems, we had to just suck it up and keep on going!" I laughed in agreement . . . but lately, more than ever, I have come to value the wisdom of his observation.

As I'm writing this chapter, Pearl and I are on the Hawaiian island of Maui. It's our first time to visit this land of love and friendship. We made this trip the old fashioned way: we earned it. The seventy-five thousand flight miles I've logged on American Airlines, traveling to conferences and Bible classes, enabled us to qualify for some no-cost transportation, discount hotel rates, and free car rental, so we thought we'd take advantage of the freebies and vacation here. (Now we're trying to think of a way that we can stay here . . . but we're not sure our executive board will go for the idea of Maui Ministries, Inc.!)

I am sitting just outside our hotel room, on a grassy ledge overlooking the sparkling blue-green Pacific. Waves roll in and shatter against the black lava rocks of the shore, sending up a fine white mist. And it occurs to me that often the lives of men and women end up just like those disintegrating waves.

When I'm out on tour, I encounter many men each week who drive their Porsches, flash their Rolexes, and spend their spare time in tanning salons and health studios, trying to firm up sagging muscles. Many have divorced their wife and left their children. Several are trying to find happiness with a young woman thirty years or so their junior. The new lifestyle may seem mighty attractive on the surface, but it doesn't fulfill. Underneath it all, one often detects the soul of a little boy asking, "Is that all there is?"

And the sense of lingering dissatisfaction is there because through divorce these men gave up what had been precious in their life, exchanging the momentary ills for temporary thrills. How different it would be if they had followed my dad's advice, determining to resolve the problems in their marriage and to keep on keeping on, no matter what.

WAY'S TO REACH THE FINISH

Any Olympic athlete will tell you that gold medals come as a result of the four D's: *desire, discipline, dedication,* and *determination.* Paul speaks of this in 1 Corinthians 9:25: "Everyone who competes in the games goes into strict training. They do it to get a crown that will not last; but we [as Christians] do it to get a crown that will last forever" (NIV). Winning a gold medal in the race of marriage demands strict training also, necessitating desire, discipline, dedication, and determination.

Hebrews 11, often called the great scriptural "hall of faith," contains the names of such triumphant believers as Abraham, Sarah, Isaac, Jacob, Joseph, and Moses. Adversity often struck the lives of the saints of Hebrews 11 (see 11:35-38), but through desire, discipline, dedication, and determination, they made it—faith intact—to the finish line anyway.

Tough times will strike our marriage too, but the words of the writer of the Hebrews can minister to us as we hit the snags and snares of matrimony:

> Therefore, since we are surrounded by such a great cloud of witnesses, let us throw off everything that hinders and the sin that so easily entangles, and let us run with perseverance the race marked out for us (Hebrews 12:1 NIV).

And the key to our being able to "run with perseverance the race marked out for us" in life, even married life, is revealed by the writer of Hebrews in the next verses of that book:

> Let us fix our eyes on Jesus, the author and perfecter of our faith, who for the joy set before him endured the cross, scorning its shame, and sat down at the right hand of the throne of God. Consider him who endured such opposition from sinful men, so that you will not grow weary and lose heart (Hebrews 12:2-3 NIV).

When we "grow weary and lose heart," we should stop to consider. We must consider Christ in all His earthly shame and Christ in all His heavenly glory. We must fix our hope on Him, both for our eternal victory and, in the meantime, for the ability to meet the day-to-day challenges of life.

Marriage has been described as an unconditional commitment to an imperfect person. Is it not logical, then, that we must look to the perfect Person in order to finish the race well? How tragic it is when anyone, especially a Christian, calls a premature halt to a marriage. For those who stop and surrender in mid-race, the question posed in Galatians 5:7 is devastatingly appropriate, "You were running well; who hindered you from obeying the truth?" (NASB).

But Is It too Late?

If you are reading these pages and saying to yourself, "It's too late for me. I've already failed," let me offer you a dose of Philippians 3:12-14. There the apostle Paul teaches us to put the past behind us—and press on, starting today.

> Not that I have already obtained all this, or have already been made perfect, but I press on to take hold of that for which Christ Jesus took hold of me. Brothers, I do not consider myself yet to have taken hold of it. But one thing I do: Forgetting what is behind and straining toward what is ahead, I press on toward the goal to win the prize for which God has called me heavenward in Christ Jesus (NIV).

Every day is a brand new day, and we must remember that the race is not always to the swift but to those who keep on running. If you think it's too late for your marriage, think again. Come before the Lord with your spouse; let God pick up the pieces and put them in place. Then get on with life—together. Even if it seems impossible for you to go for the gold, remember that you still have the golden streets of eternity ahead of you!

As we walk, skip, run, or even plod along the road to those golden streets, the words of Isaiah 40:28-31 serve to encourage and challenge us. The verses exhort us to rely upon God's strength as we approach our final destination:

Do you not know?
  Have you not heard?
The LORD is the everlasting God,
  the Creator of the ends of the earth.
He will not grow tired or weary,
  and his understanding no one can fathom.
He gives strength to the weary
  and increases the power of the weak.
Even youths grow tired and weary,
  and young men stumble and fall;
but those who hope in the LORD
  will renew their strength.
They will soar on wings like eagles;
  they will run and not grow weary,
  they will walk and not be faint (NIV).

ON OUR WAY

Maui is agreeing with Pearl and me. The warm sun feels
good on my arthritic hip. People say old age creeps up on
you but in my case, it came on at a dead run. I think I
really will see if they can't use an aging Bible teacher
around here. It looks like a great place to go out in a blaze
of glory!

Pearl and I have made it thirty-three years together;
seventeen more takes us to the gold. It's wonderful to have
five children who love us, two little guys who call us
Grandma and Grandpa, and most of all, each other. The
Lord really does things in a grand way when we follow His
lead and hang in there when so many others around us are
dropping like flies.

Our fiftieth anniversary should be something special. I
think I'll see if I can hire Kenny Rogers to perform for the
occasion . . . but only if he'll consent to sing this song,
entitled "Through the Years":

  I can't remember when you weren't there,
  When I ever cared for anyone but you.
  I swear, we've been through everything there is,

I can't imagine anything we've missed,
I can't imagine anything the two of us can't do.

And through the years, you've never let me down,
You've turned my life around,
The sweetest days I've found I've found with you.
Through the years I've never been afraid,
I've loved the life we've made,
I'm very glad I've stayed right here with you,
Through the years.

I can't remember what I used to do,
Who I trusted, who I listened to before.
I swear, you've taught me everything I know,
I can't imagine needing someone so,
But through the years it seems to me
I need you more and more.

And through the years through all the good and bad,
I knew how much we've had,
I've always been so glad to be with you.
Through the years it's better every day.
You've kissed my tears away.
As long as it's okay I'll stay with you
Through the years.

And through the years when everything went wrong
Together we were strong,
I knew that I belonged right here with you.
Through the years I never had a doubt
We'd always work things out,
I've learned what life's about by loving you
Through the years.

And through the years you've never let me down.
You've turned my life around.
The sweetest days I've found I've found with you.
Through the years it's better every day.
You've kissed my tears away.
As long as it's okay I'll stay with you
Through the years.

Suggested Readings

ON THE SONG OF SOLOMON:

Bolchin, John A. 1970. "The Song of Solomon." In *The New Bible Commentary: Revised*. Grand Rapids, Michigan: William B. Eerdmans Publishing Company.

Carr, G. Lloyd. 1984. *The Song of Solomon: An Introduction and Commentary*. The Tyndale Old Testament Commentaries. Downers Grove, Illinois: InterVarsity Press.

Deere, Jack S. 1985. "Song of Songs." In *The Bible Knowledge Commentary: Old Testament*. Wheaton, Illinois: Victor Books.

Dillow, Joseph C. *Solomon on Sex*. 1977. New York: Thomas Nelson Publishers, Inc.

Glickman, S. Craig. 1976. *A Song for Lovers*. Downers Grove, Illinois: InterVarsity Press.

Hocking, David, and Carole Hocking. 1986. *Romantic Lovers*. Eugene, Oregon: Harvest House Publishers.

Ironside, H.A. 1933. *Addresses on the Song of Solomon*. Neptune, New Jersey: Loizeaux Brothers.

Patterson, Paige. 1985. "The Song of Solomon." In *Everyman's Bible Commentary*. Wheaton, Illinois: Moody Press.

ON MARRIAGE:

Barber, Cyril, and Aldyth Barber. 1982. *Your Marriage Has Real Possibilities*. San Bernadino, California: Here's Life Publishers, Inc.

Crabb, Lawrence J. 1982. *The Marriage Builder*. Grand Rapids, Michigan: Zondervan Publishing House.

Dobson, James C. 1983. *Love Must Be Tough*. Waco, Texas: Word Books.

———. 1980. *Straight Talk to Men and Their Wives*. Waco, Texas: Word Books.

———. 1975. *What Wives Wish Their Husbands Knew about Women*. Wheaton, Illinois: Tyndale House Publishers.

Field, David. 1986. *Marriage Personalities*. Eugene, Oregon: Harvest House Publishers.

Fritze, J.A. 1969. *The Essence of Marriage*. Grand Rapids, Michigan: Zondervan Publishing House.

Getz, Gene A. 1980. *The Measure of a Marriage*. Ventura, California: Regal Books.

MacDonald, Gordon. 1976. *Magnificent Marriage*. Wheaton, Illinois: Tyndale House Publishers.

Roberts, Patti, and Sherry Andrews. 1983. *Ashes to Gold*. Waco, Texas: Word Books.

Sell, Charles M. 1982. *Achieving the Impossible: Intimate Marriage*. Portland, Oregon: Multnomah Press.

Shedd, Charlie W. 1968. *Letters to Karen: On Keeping Love in Marriage*. New York: Avon Books, Spire Edition.

———. 1978. *Letters to Philip: On How to Treat a Woman*. Old Tappan, New Jersey: Fleming H. Revell, Spire Books.

Smalley, Gary, and Steve Scott. 1982. *For Better or Best*. Revised edition. Grand Rapids, Michigan: Zondervan Publishing House.

———. 1979. *If Only He Knew*. Grand Rapids, Michigan: Zondervan Publishing House.

Thomas, Terry C. 1979. *At Least We Were Married*. Grand Rapids, Michigan: Zondervan Publishing House.

Timmons, Tim. 1976. *Maximum Marriage*. Old Tappan, New Jersey: Fleming H. Revell Company, Power Books.

Vanauken, Sheldon. 1977. *A Severe Mercy*. New York: Harper and Row, Publishers, Inc..

Wheat, Ed, M.D. and Gaye Wheat. 1981. *Intended for Pleasure*. Old Tappan, New Jersey: Fleming H. Revell Company.

———. 1980. *Love-Life for Every Married Couple*. Grand Rapids, Michigan: Zondervan Publishing House.

Williams, Pat, Jill Williams, and Jerry Jenkins. 1985. *Rekindled*. Old Tappan, New Jersey: Fleming H. Revell Company.

Acknowledgments

Baker, Mark. 1981. *NAM The Vietnam War in the Words of the Men and Women Who Fought There.* New York: William Morrow and Company, Inc. Copyright 1981 by Mark Baker. Used by permission.

Calkin, Ruth Harms. 1986. *Marriage Is So Much More, Lord.* Wheaton, Illinois: Tyndale House Publishers, Inc., Living Books. Used by permission.

Dillow, Joseph C. 1977. *Solomon on Sex.* Nashville, Tennessee: Thomas Nelson Publishers, Inc.

Dobson, James C. 1975. *What Wives Wish Their Husbands Knew about Women.* Wheaton, Illinois: Tyndale House Publishers, Inc.

Dorff, Steve, and Marty Panzer. 1981. "Through the Years." PESO MUSIC (BMI)/SwaneeBRAVO! Music (BMI). Used by permission.

Glickman, S. Craig. 1976. *A Song for Lovers.* Downers Grove, Illinois: InterVarsity Press. Copyright 1976 by InterVarsity Christian Fellowship of the USA and used by permission of InterVarsity Press, P.O. Box 1400, Downers, Grove, IL 60515.

Hocking, David, and Carole Hocking. 1986. *Romantic Lovers.* Eugene, Oregon: Harvest House Publishers.

Ironside, H. A. 1981. *Proverbs and the Song of Solomon.* Neptune, New Jersey: Loiuzeaux Brothers, Inc. Used by permission.

Lear, Martha Weinman. "How Many Choices Do Women Really Have?" *Woman's Day,* 11 November 1986.

Lerner, Alan Jay, and Frederick Loewe. 1967. "How to Handle a Woman," from *Camelot.* Chapell & Company, Inc. Copyright 1960 by Alan Jay Lerner and Frederick Loewe. Chappell & Co., Inc., owner of publication and allied rights throughout the world. International copyright secured. All rights reserved. Used by permission.

Roberts, Patti, and Sherry Andrews. 1983. *Ashes to Gold*. Waco, Texas: Word Books. Copyright 1983, used by permission of Word Books, publisher.

Rogers, Kenny. 1981. "Through the Years." Hollywood: Liberty Records. Used by permission.

Ryrie, Charles C. 1986. *Basic Theology*. Wheaton, Illinois: Victor Books. Used by permission.

Segal, Brenda Lesley. 1980. *The Tenth Measure*. New York: St. Martin's Press.

Shedd, Charlie. 1978. *Letters to Philip: On How to Treat a Woman*. Old Tappan, New Jersey: Fleming H. Revell Company, Spire Books. Copyright 1968 by Charles W. Shedd and the Abundance Foundation. Reprinted by permission of Doubleday Company, Inc.

Thomas, Terry C. 1979. *At Least We Were Married*. Grand Rapids, Michigan: Zondervan Publishing House. Copyright 1970 by Zondervan Publishing House. Used by permission.

Timmons, Tim. 1976. *Maximum Marriage*. Old Tappan, New Jersey: Fleming H. Revell Company, Power Books. Copyright 1976 by Fleming H. Revell Company. Used by permission.

Unger, Merrill F. 1983. *Principles of Expository Preaching*. Grand Rapids, Michigan: Zondervan Corporation. Copyright 1955, 1983 by Zondervan Publishing house. Used by permission.

Vanauken, Sheldon. 1977. *A Severe Mercy*. New York: Harper and Row, Publishers, Inc. Copyright 1977, 1980 by Sheldon Vanauken. Reprinted by permission of Harper and Row, Publishers, Inc.

Williams, Pat, Jill Williams, and Jerry Jenkins. 1985. *Rekindled*. Old Tappan, New Jersey: Fleming H. Revell Company. Copyright 1985 by Patrick L. M. Williams and Jill M. P. Williams and Jerry Jenkins. Used by permission.

DON ANDERSON MINISTRIES

Popular pastor, teacher, and conference speaker, Don Anderson tours Texas and neighboring states giving Bible classes and business luncheon seminars during the fall, winter, and spring months. During the summer, Don Anderson Ministries staffs many youth and family camps. Don also preaches regularly at two churches staffed by the Ministries and speaks at conferences in various locations in the United States and Canada. His audiences of business and professional men and women, housewives and trades-people, testify that his refreshing teaching makes the Scriptures "come alive" for them.

Don Anderson graduated from Northwestern College in 1955 with a bachelor of arts degree and received his master's degree from Dallas Theological Seminary. He has been in Christian ministry for over thirty years serving as a Young Life staff member, youth pastor, program director at the Firs Bible and Missionary Conference, executive director of Pine Cove Conference Center, and, since 1972, has served as director of the non-profit organization, Don Anderson Ministries, headquartered in Tyler, Texas.

Don Anderson has many audio and video cassette tapes based on his teachings which are produced by the Ministries and distributed widely. There is also a Ministries newsletter, *The Grapevine*, which reaches about eight thousand homes.

If you'd like to enhance your study of the Scriptures, the cassette tape series of *Make Full My Joy* is available from the author. If you are interested in hearing Don's teachings, please write to this address for a free tape catalog.

Don Anderson Ministries
Station A, Box 6611
Tyler, Texas 75711